P9-CKY-102

THE ULTIMATE
FAT-FREE
DESSERT
COOKBOOK

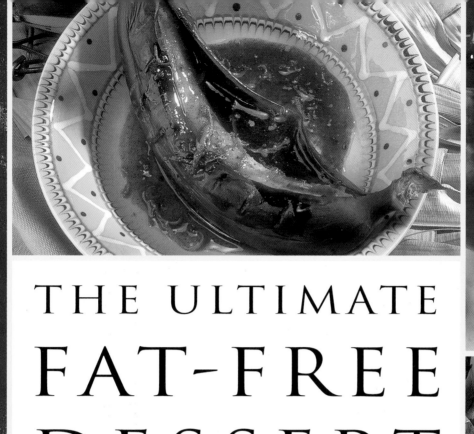

THE ULTIMATE
FAT-FREE
DESSERT
COOKBOOK

The BEST-EVER STEP-BY-STEP

COLLECTION *of* NO-FAT *and*

LOW-FAT RECIPES *for* EXCITING,

SATISFYING *and* HEALTHY EATING

CONSULTING EDITOR: WENDY DOYLE

LORENZ BOOKS

First published in 1999 by Lorenz Books
27 West 20th Street, New York, NY 10011

LORENZ BOOKS available for bulk purchase for sales promotion and for premium use.
For details, write or call the sales director,
Lorenz Books, 27 West 20th Street, New York, NY 10011; (800) 354-9657.

© 1999 Anness Publishing Limited

Lorenz Books is an imprint of
Anness Publishing Inc.

This edition distributed in Canada by
Raincoast Books
8680 Cambie Street, Vancouver
British Columbia V6P 6M9

This edition published in 1999 for Index

All rights reserved. No part of this publication may be reproduced, stored in a retrieval system, or transmitted in any way or by any
means, electronic, mechanical, photocopying, recording or otherwise, without the prior written permission of the copyright holder.

ISBN 1 85967 909 9

Publisher: Joanna Lorenz
Managing Editor: Helen Sudell
Editor: Jenni Fleetwood
Production Controller: Ann Childers
Editorial Reader: Joy Wotton
Designer: Nigel Partridge
Recipes: Catherine Atkinson, Alex Barker, Michelle Berriedale-Johnson, Angela Boggiano, Janet Brinkworth, Carla Capalbo, Jacqueline Clark,
Frances Cleary, Carol Clements, Roz Denny, Patrizia Diemling, Nicola Diggins, Joanna Farrow, Christine France, Sarah Gates, Shirly Gill,
Rosamund Grant, Carole Handslip, Deh-Ta Hsiung, Shehzad Husain, Sheila Kimberley, Gilly Love, Sue Maggs, Maggie Mayhew, Maggie Parnell,
Anne Sheasby, Liz Trigg, Laura Washburn, Steven Wheeler, Kate Whiteman, Elizabeth Wolf-Cohen, Jeni Wright
Photographers: William Adams-Lingwood, Karl Adamson, Edward Allwright, David Armstrong, Steve Baxter, James Duncan,
Michelle Garrett, Amanda Heywood, David Jordan, Don Last, Patrick McLeavey, Michael Michaels, Thomas Odulate

Printed in Italy

1 3 5 7 9 10 8 6 4 2

PUBLISHER'S NOTE
The nutritional analysis of recipes excludes all optional items and serving suggestions.

FACTS ABOUT FATS

We all know we need to cut down on the amount of fat we eat—it would be difficult to live in the world and be unaware of that fact—but before making changes in our diet, it may be helpful to find out a bit more about the fats that we eat: some types are believed to be less harmful than others.

Fats are essential for the proper functioning of the body. However, we need the right kind of fat and the right amount. The average Western diet contains far too much of the "wrong" type of fat—saturated fat—which leads to obesity, heart problems and strokes. The daily recommended maximum amount of calories that should come from fat is between 30 and 35%. Unfortunately, many Westerners obtain well over 40% of their calories from fat, often in the form of sweet treats and desserts and pastries.

Fats in our food are made up of different types of fatty acids and glycerol. Fats may be saturated or unsaturated, with unsaturated fat further categorized as mono-unsaturated or polyunsaturated.

SATURATED FATS

To appreciate the difference between saturated and unsaturated fatty acids, it is necessary to understand a little about their molecular structure. Put very simply, fatty acids are made up of chains of carbon atoms. A common analogy is to a string of beads. Unlike beads, however, which are linked only to each other, the carbon atoms are also able to link up—or bond—with one or more other atoms. In a saturated fat, all these potential linkages have been made: the carbon atoms are linked to each other and each is further linked to two hydrogen atoms.

LEFT: A bottle of sunflower oil (left) contains mostly polyunsaturated fats (68%), while olive oil is made of up mainly mono-unsaturated fats (70%).

No further linkages are possible, and the fat is therefore said to be saturated.

Saturated fat is mainly found in foods of animal origin: meat and dairy products such as butter, which become solid at room temperature. However, there are also some saturated fats of vegetable origin, notably coconut oil and palm oil.

UNSATURATED FATS

Unsaturated fatty acids differ from saturated fatty acids in their structure—not all of the linkages or bonds are complete. Some of the carbon atoms are linked to only one hydrogen atom instead of the usual two, and some of the carbon atoms may be joined to each other by a double bond. Depending on how many double bonds there are, the fatty acid is described as mono-unsaturated (one double bond) or polyunsaturated (many double bonds). All the ramifications of these different molecular structures need not concern us here—suffice it to say that unsaturated fats are generally healthier than saturated fats.

MONOUNSATURATED FATS

These are found in foods such as olive oil, canola oil, some nuts, oily fish and avocados. Monounsaturated fats are believed to be neutral, neither raising or lowering blood cholesterol levels. This, plus the fact that people in Mediterranean countries tend to have a much lower saturated fat intake as well as eating more fruit and vegetables, which are high in antioxidants, could explain why there is such a low incidence of heart disease in these countries.

ABOVE: Many common foods contain some fats. Cheese, butter, milk, cream and nuts —all of which are frequently used in desserts—should be strictly limited, unless fat free or very low fat.

POLYUNSATURATED FATS

There are two types of polyunsaturated fats. The first (omega 6) is found in vegetable and seed oils, such as sunflower or almond oil, and the second (omega 3) comes from oily fish, green leaves and some seed oils, including canola oil.

Polyunsaturated fats are liquid at room temperature. When vegetable oils are used in the manufacture of soft margarine, they have to be hardened artificially. During this process, the composition of some of the unsaturated fatty acids changes. In the body, these altered or "trans" fatty acids are treated like saturated fats, so, although an oil such as sunflower oil may be high in polyunsaturated fatty acids, the same is not necessarily true of a margarine made from that oil. The only way to find out is to check the label.

Polyunsaturated fats lower cholesterol levels. Although unsaturated fats are more healthy than saturated ones, most experts agree that what matters more is that we all reduce our total intake of fat.

A GUIDE TO LOW-FAT DESSERT INGREDIENTS

Watching your fat intake doesn't mean you have to forgo creamy desserts. A wide range of low-fat and virtually fat-free products are on sale in supermarkets, some of them backed by alluring advertising. Clever packaging can sometimes persuade the impulse buyer to make an unwise choice, however, so always check the statistical data printed on the label.

Low-fat spreads have become very popular. These have a high water content, so, while they are perfectly acceptable for spreading on bread and teabreads, they are not necessarily suitable for cooking. When baking desserts or making cakes, look for a spread with a fat content of around 40%. If substituting a reduced-fat spread for butter in a conventional recipe, be prepared to experiment a little, as the results will not be the same.

Avoid using saturated fats such as butter and hard margarine. Oils that are high in polyunsaturates, such as sunflower, corn or safflower, are the healthier option. Cakes and baked goods made with oil can be excellent. If you must use margarine, choose a brand that is low in saturates and high in polyunsaturates.

Skim milk works well in batters, although you may get a better result using low-fat milk. Yogurt and fromage frais make excellent alternatives to cream, and when combined with honey, liqueur or other flavorings, they make delicious fillings or toppings for cheesecakes and fruit desserts. Many delectable desserts are based on soft cheeses. Cream cheese used to be the preferred option, but low-fat alternatives work just as well and are often easier to mix. If you're not familiar with it already, experiment with Quark, a virtually fat-free cheese that is very versatile.

OILS AND LOW-FAT SPREADS

CORN OIL: A polyunsaturated oil, this has a slight flavor, so it is not as good as sunflower oil for baking. Fried foods should be avoided completely if you are trying to limit your fat intake, but if you must fry this is a good choice, because it can reach a high temperature without smoking.

SUNFLOWER OIL SPREAD: High in polyunsaturates, this light, delicately flavored oil is a good choice for desserts, as is safflower oil. Both can be used in cakes and are particularly good in muffins.

SUNFLOWER LIGHT SPREAD: Like reduced-fat butter, this contains about 38% fat, plus emulsified milk solids and water. The flavor is mild.

LEFT: A selection of cooking oils and low-fat spreads. Always check the packaging when buying low-fat spreads—if you are going to use them for cooking, they must have a fat content of about 40%.

LOW-FAT SPREAD (rich buttermilk blend): This product is made with a high proportion of buttermilk, which is naturally low in fat. Low-fat spreads with a fat content of around 40% can be used for cooking; check the label.

VERY LOW-FAT SPREAD: This contains about 20–30% fat and has a high water content; it is not suitable for cooking.

LOW-FAT MILKS

BUTTERMILK: Real buttermilk is the liquid that remains after cream has been churned into butter. Buttermilk produced in this way has a light flavor, similar to skim milk. Commercial buttermilk is made by adding a bacterial culture to skim milk. This gives it a slightly sharper taste than traditional buttermilk. It is very low in fat (0.5%).

POWDERED SKIM MILK: This is a useful low-fat standby. You can make up as little or as much as you need. Always follow the instructions on the package. The powder itself has quite a high fat content, so if you use too much, the milk will not be the low-fat alternative you wanted.

LOW-FAT MILK: With a fat content between 1% and 2%, this milk doesn't taste as rich as full-cream milk. It is favored by many people for everyday use for precisely this reason. Low-fat milk can be used in all recipes calling for full-cream milk.

SKIM MILK: This milk has had virtually all the fat removed, leaving 0.1%. It is ideal for those wishing to reduce their intake of fats.

LOW-FAT CREAM SUBSTITUTES

CRÈME FRAÎCHE: Look out for low-fat versions of this thick soured cream, where

ABOVE: Almost all dairy products now come in low-fat or reduced-fat versions.

the normal fat content of 40% is reduced to 15%. Crème fraîche has a mild, lemony taste and is ideal as a topping.

PLAIN YOGURT: This thick, creamy yogurt is made from whole milk with a fat content of 9.1%. Low-fat versions are also available.

LOW-FAT PLAIN YOGURT: With a fat content of only about 1%, low-fat plain yogurt is a gift to the dessert cook. Use it instead of cream in whips, as a topping or as an accompaniment. Drizzle a little honey on top if you like.

LOW-FAT CHEESES

COTTAGE CHEESE: This low-fat cheese is also available in a low-fat form. Cottage cheese can be used instead of cream cheese in cheesecakes—press it through a sieve to remove the lumps.

CURD CHEESE: This low-fat soft cheese is generally made from skim or low-fat milk. A simple version can be made at home, using low-fat plain yogurt. Use curd cheese instead of cream cheese.

EDAM: Hard cheeses are not widely used in desserts, except in some baked cheesecakes. If a recipe does call for grated hard cheese, however, this is a good choice as it is lower in fat than standards like Cheddar or Cheshire. If you prefer the taste of Cheddar, choose a reduced-fat version.

FROMAGE FRAIS: This is a fresh, soft cheese with a very mild flavor. It is available in two grades: virtually fat-free (0.2% fat), and a more creamy variety (7.1% fat). Fromage frais is too soft to use on its own as a cheesecake filling, but it can be mixed with curd cheese.

QUARK: Perfect for many different types of dessert, this soft white cheese is virtually fat-free. It is made from fermented skim milk.

FAT AND CALORIE COUNTS PER 100g

The chart below lists both full-fat and low or reduced-fat typical dessert ingredients, so that
you can see the savings at a glance if you choose the healthier option.

INGREDIENT	FAT (G)	CALORIES	INGREDIENT	FAT (G)	CALORIES
OILS AND SPREADS			Curd cheese	11.7	173
Butter	81.7	737	Edam	25	333
Corn oil	99.9	899	Fromage frais (plain)	7.1	113
Low-fat spread	40.5	390	Low-fat Cheddar	15	261
Margarine	81.6	739	Quark	1.4	86
Olive oil	99.9	899	Reduced-fat cottage cheese	1.4	78
Olive oil reduced-fat spread	63	571	Very low-fat fromage frais	0.2	58
Safflower oil	99.9	899			
Sunflower oil	99.9	899	**EGGS**		
Sunflower light spread	38	357	about 2 (medium)	10.9	147
Very low-fat spread	27	259	Egg white	trace	36
			Egg yolk	30.5	339
MILK					
Buttermilk	0.5	37	**BAKING PRODUCTS AND PRESERVES**		
Low-fat milk	1.6	46	Chocolate (milk)	30.3	520
Skim milk	0.1	33	Chocolate (unsweetened)	29.2	510
Skim milk powder	0.6	348	Cocoa powder	21.7	359
Whole milk	3.9	66	Fat-free sponge cake	6.1	294
			Honey	0	288
CREAM/CREAM SUBSTITUTES			Sugar (white)	0	394
Crème fraîche	40	380			
Heavy cream	48	449	**FRUIT AND NUTS**		
Low-fat crème fraîche	15	166	Almonds	55.8	612
Low-fat yogurt (plain)	0.8	56	Apples	0.1	47
Plain yogurt	9.1	115	Bananas	0.3	95
Light cream	19.1	198	Brazil nuts	68.2	68.2
Whipping cream	39.3	373	Dried mixed fruit	0.4	268
			Hazelnuts	63.5	650
CHEESES			Oranges	0.1	37
Cheddar	34.4	412	Peaches	0.1	33
Cottage cheese (plain)	3.9	98	Peanut butter (smooth)	53.7	623
Cream cheese	47.7	439	Pears	0.1	40
			Pine nuts	68.6	688

Information from *The Composition of Foods* (5th edition 1991) is reproduced with the permission
of the Controller of Her Majesty's Stationery Office.

MAKING DESSERTS THE FAT-FREE WAY

To many people, dessert means lots of cream, butter and chocolate. Nowdays, however, it is perfectly possible for a host to hoodwink guests into thinking they are having a luscious, creamy sweet, when all the while, the constituents are fat-free or low in fat.

Many ingredients are available in reduced-fat or very low-fat forms. In every supermarket you'll find a huge array of low-fat products, such as milk, cream, yogurt, hard and soft cheeses and fromage frais, reduced-fat sweet or chocolate cookies; low-fat or very low-fat spreads; as well as reduced-fat prepared desserts. Some ingredients work better than others in cooking, but often a simple substitution will spell success. In a crumb crust, for instance, reduced-fat cookies work just as well as classic one.

Some of the most delicious desserts are based on fruit. Serve fresh or dried fruit in a salad or compote, and there's absolutely no need to introduce fats. If you are making a baked or steamed pudding, or pan-frying fruit such as bananas or pineapple rings, you can get away with using a slick of polyunsaturated oil, especially if you use a non-stick pan. Alternatively, use spray oil: a one-second spray of sunflower oil (about $1/5$ of a teaspoon) has 4.6 calories and just over half the fat of conventional cooking oil. Spray oil is particularly useful for lightly coating frying pans when making pancakes or crêpes.

When seeking inspiration for the dessert course for that special dinner party, remember that there are plenty of ingredients that naturally contain very little fat. Rice, flour, oatmeal, bread and cornflakes can all be used to make desserts and toppings, and there's no fat in wine, sherry, sugar or honey, although you may wish to restrict these for other reasons! Meringues are among the most popular desserts— topped with fresh fruit and yogurt or fromage frais, they are irresistible to eat and look great.

Spices and extracts add plenty of extra flavor and color to desserts, while decorations like rose petals, mint leaves or curls of pared citrus zest improve the appearance and stimulate the appetite.

LOW-FAT SPREADS IN COOKING
Some low-fat spreads can safely be substituted for butter or margarine in baked desserts, but others are only suitable for spreading. The limiting factor is the amount of water in the product. Very low-fat spreads achieve levels of fat of around 20% by virtue of their high water content and cannot be melted successfully. Spreads with a fat content of around 40% are suitable for spreading and for some cooking methods.

RIGHT: This sumptuous pineapple and strawberry marshmallow meringue looks and tastes delicious even though it is very low in fat.

LEFT: Fresh fruit can be used to make simply superb sweet dishes, and there's no need at all to add any fat.

When using low-fat spreads for cooking, the fat may behave slightly differently to full-fat products such as butter or margarine. Be prepared to experiment a little – the results may surprise you. Some recipes actually work better with low-fat ingredients. For example, choux pastry made with half- or low-fat spread is often slightly crisper and lighter in texture than traditional choux pastry. A cheesecake cookie crust made with melted half- or low-fat spread combined with crumbs from reduced-fat cookies may be slightly softer in texture and less crisp than one made using melted butter, but it will still be very good.

QUICK TIPS FOR FAT-FREE COOKING

• Use heavy or nonstick pans—that way you won't need as much fat for cooking.

• When baking low-fat or reduced-fat cakes, it is advisable to use good quality cookware that doesn't need greasing before use, or line the pan with nonstick baking parchment and only grease very lightly before filling.

• Bake fruit in a loosely sealed parcel of waxed paper, moistening it with wine, fruit juice or liqueur instead of butter before sealing the parcel.

• When grilling fruit, the naturally high moisture content means that it is often unnecessary to add fat. If the fruit looks a bit dry, brush lightly and sparingly with a polyunsaturated oil such as sunflower or corn oil.

• Fruit cooked in the microwave seldom needs additional fat; add spices for extra color and flavor.

• Poach fresh or dried fruit in natural juice or syrup—there's no need to add any fat.

• Become an expert at cooking with phyllo pastry. Of itself, phyllo is extremely low in fat, and if you brush the sheets sparingly with melted low-fat spread, it can be used to make delicious desserts that will not significantly damage a low-fat diet and will replace other high-fat pastries.

• Avoid cooking with chocolate, which is high in fat. If you can't bear to abandon your favorite flavor, use reduced-fat cocoa powder instead.

• Get to know the full range of low- or reduced-fat products, including yogurt, crème fraîche and fromage frais. Low-fat yogurt can be used for making "creamy" sauces, but needs to be treated with a little more care than cream as it is liable to curdle when heated. Stabilize it by stirring in a little cornstarch, mixed to a paste with water or skim milk.

• Use skim milk rather than whole milk in rice pudding, semolina pudding and batters.

ABOVE: Many delicious desserts can be made in minutes if you have a well-stocked pantry.

When heating low-fat spreads, never let them get too hot. Always use a heavy pan over a low heat to avoid the product burning, spitting or spoiling, and stir all the time. Low-fat spreads cannot be used for shallow- or deep-frying, traditional pastry making, rich fruit cakes, shortbread and preserves such as lemon curd.

Baked goods, such as cakes, pies and pastries, made using reduced- or low-fat spreads will not keep as well as cakes and teabreads made using butter; this is due to the lower fat content.

FRUIT PURÉES

One way of reducing the fat content of a recipe is to replace all or part of the fat with a fruit purée. This is particularly successful with breads, probably because the amount of fat is usually relatively small, and it also works well with some cookies and bars, such as brownies.

To make a dried fruit purée for this purpose, roughly chop 2/3 cup dried fruit and put it in a blender or food processor. Add 5 tablespoons of water and blend to a fairly smooth purée. Scrape into a bowl, cover and keep in the refrigerator for up to 3 days. When baking, simply substitute the same volume of this dried fruit purée for all or just some of the fat in the recipe. You may need to experiment a little to find the proportions that work best. If preferred, you can purée a single variety of dried fruit, such as prunes, apricots, peaches or apples, or substitute mashed fresh fruit, such as ipe bananas or lightly cooked apples. If you choose to purée fresh fruit, omit the water.

USEFUL TECHNIQUES

BEATING EGG WHITES

1 Place the egg whites in a completely clean, grease-free bowl. If even a speck of egg yolk is present, you will not be able to beat the whites successfully. Use one half of the shell to remove any traces of yolk.

2 Use a balloon whisk in a wide bowl for the greatest volume (egg whites can increase their volume by about eight times), but an electric hand beater will also do an efficient job. Purists swear that eggs beaten in a copper bowl give the greatest volume.

3 Beat the whites until they are firm enough to hold either soft or stiff peaks when you lift the whisk—see individual recipes. For stiffly beaten whites, you should be able to hold the bowl upside down without their sliding out, but this is a risky test!

MAKING CRÊPES

1 Apply a light, even coat of spray oil to a 8-inch pan, then heat it gently. Pour in about 3 tablespoons of the batter, then quickly tilt the pan so that the batter spreads to cover the bottom thinly and evenly.

2 Cook the crêpe for 30-45 seconds, until it has set. Carefully lift the edge with a spatula; the bottom of the crêpe should have browned lightly. Shake the pan to loosen the crêpe, then turn it over or flip it with a quick twist of your wrist.

3 Cook the other side of the crêpe for about 30 seconds, then slide the crêpe out onto a plate. Make more crêpes in the same way, then spread them with your chosen filling before rolling them or folding them neatly into triangles.

INTRODUCTION

All too often, dessert is the downfall of the person trying to follow a low-fat diet. After a sensible appetizer and a main course composed of grilled fish or chicken and fresh vegetables, there's an almost irresistible temptation to award yourself a large portion of dessert.

The good news is that you can. You don't have to give up delicious desserts—provided you stick to the recipes in this book. Carefully designed to fit into a healthy, lighter diet, each has no more than 5 grams of fat per portion, and many have fewer than 200 calories.

The secret of eating for good health is making sure that your diet has a good nutritional balance. Cutting down on fat but increasing sugar is not the solution, so while these desserts bring a little sweetness into our lives, many of them do so by using small amounts of honey or the natural sugars present in fresh and dried fruits.

We all know we should be eating more fruit—it is recommended that we eat five portions of fresh fruit or vegetables each day—so fresh fruit desserts score on a variety of levels, not only supplying sweetness, but also contributing fiber, essential vitamins and minerals. These recipes make full use of the wonderfully abundant choice of fruits we now have all year round.

We are also lucky to have available lots of delicious, lighter alternatives to ingredients such as cream—so even classic rich dishes can be lightened quite easily. You'll find that, after a while, your tastes will change, and in many cases you will actually prefer the lighter, fresher flavors of low-fat desserts to some of the over-rich alternatives.

So whether you are aiming to eat less fat in order to lose weight, or just trying to eat more healthy, this book will help you do so without giving up the sweet things in life.

RIGHT: For healthy desserts, make use of the natural sweetness and color of fruit.

CONTENTS

DISSOLVING GELATIN

1 Powdered gelatin is very easy to use. For every 1 tablespoon of gelatin in the recipe, place 3 tablespoons of very hot water in a small bowl.

2 Holding the bowl steady, sprinkle the powdered gelatin lightly and evenly over the hot liquid. Always add the gelatin to the liquid; never the other way round.

3 Stir until the gelatin has dissolved completely and the liquid is clear, with no visible crystals. You may need to stand the bowl in a pan of hot water.

UNMOLDING A JELLY

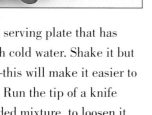

1 Have ready a serving plate that has been rinsed with cold water. Shake it but leave it damp—this will make it easier to center the jelly. Run the tip of a knife around the molded mixture, to loosen it.

2 Dip the mold briefly into a bowl of hot water. One or two seconds is usually enough—if you leave it for too long, the mixture will start to melt around the edges. If the jelly is stuck, dip again. Several short dips are better than one long one.

3 Quickly invert the plate over the mold. Holding mold and plate together, turn both over. Shake firmly to dislodge the jelly; as soon as you feel it drop, lift off the mold. If it does not lift off, give it another shake.

QUICK TIPS FOR GELATIN

Dissolving gelatin in cold liquid: Some recipes require gelatin to be dissolved in a cold liquid, such as apple or orange juice. In this case, pour the liquid into a small heatproof bowl and sprinkle the gelatin on top. Set aside until the liquid has absorbed the gelatin and looks spongy, then place the bowl over very hot water until the gelatin has dissolved completely. You could either use a *bain marie* or simply a pan full of boiling water.

TECHNIQUES FOR TASTY TOPPINGS

Low-fat Whipped "Cream"

INGREDIENTS

1/2 teaspoon powdered gelatin
5 tablespoons water
1/4 cup skim milk powder
1 tablespoon sugar
1 tablespoon lemon juice

MAKES 2/3 CUP

1 Sprinkle the powdered gelatin over 1 tablespoon cold water in a small bowl and let "sponge" for 5 minutes. Place the bowl over a pan of hot water and stir until dissolved. Let cool.

2 Beat the milk powder, sugar, lemon juice and remaining water until frothy. Add the dissolved gelatin and whisk. Chill for 30 minutes.

3 Using an electric hand beater, beat the chilled mixture again until it holds its shape and is very thick and frothy. Serve within 30 minutes of making.

Yogurt Piping Cream

INGREDIENTS

2 teaspoons powdered gelatin
3 tablespoons water
1 1/4 cups strained yogurt
1 tablespoon fructose
1/2 teaspoon vanilla extract
1 egg white

MAKES SCANT 2 CUPS

1 Sprinkle the gelatin over the water in a small bowl and let "sponge" for 5 minutes. Place the bowl over a saucepan of hot water and stir until dissolved. Let cool.

2 Mix together the yogurt, fructose and vanilla extract. Stir in the gelatin. Chill in the refrigerator for 30 minutes, or until just beginning to set around the edges.

3 Beat the egg white until stiff, then carefully fold it into the yogurt mixture. Spoon into a piping bag fitted with a piping nozzle and use immediately.

STRAINED YOGURT AND SIMPLE CURD CHEESE

INGREDIENTS

2 cups low-fat yogurt

MAKES 1 1/4 CUPS
STRAINED YOGURT OR
1/2 CUP CURD CHEESE

1 For strained yogurt, line a nylon or stainless steel sieve with a double layer of muslin. Put it over a bowl and carefully pour in the low-fat yogurt.

2 Let drain in the refrigerator for 3 hours, by which time it will have separated into thick strained yogurt and watery whey. Discard the whey.

3 For curd cheese, let drain in the refrigerator for 8 hours or overnight. Spoon the curd cheese into a serving bowl, cover and keep chilled until needed.

APRICOT GLAZE

1 Place a few spoonfuls of apricot jam in a small pan and add a squeeze of lemon juice. Heat the jam, stirring until it has melted and is runny.

2 Set a wire sieve over a heatproof bowl. Pour the jam into the sieve, then stir it with a wooden spoon to help it go through the mesh.

3 Return the strained jam to the pan. Keep the glaze warm until needed, then brush it generously over the fresh fruit until evenly coated.

DECORATING WITH CITRUS ZEST SHREDS

Shredded citrus zest makes a very effective decoration for a low-fat dessert. Thinly pare the zest from an orange, lemon or lime, using a swivel vegetable peeler. Take care not to remove any of the white pith, which is bitter. Cut the strips of pared zest into very fine shreds with a sharp knife. Boil the shreds for a couple of minutes in water or sugar syrup to soften them.

RIGHT: The shredded zest of oranges, lemons and limes add extra color and appeal to this simple citrus jelly.

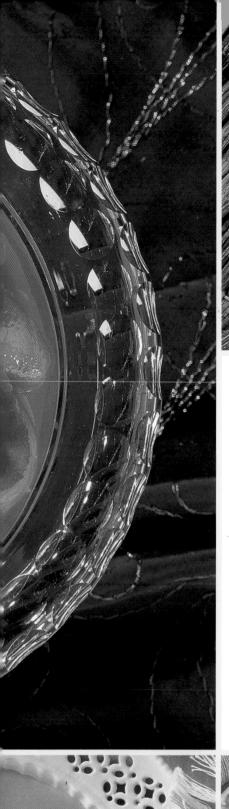

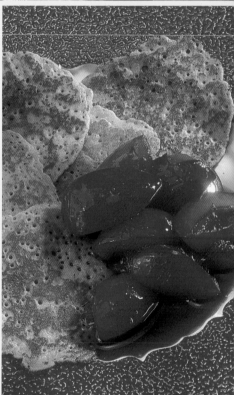

HOT FRUIT
DESSERTS

Banish winter chills with soul-warming desserts
full of autumn's bountiful harvest of fruits, or add
spice to a summer evening's *al fresco* dinner party
with luxurious yet low-fat desserts.

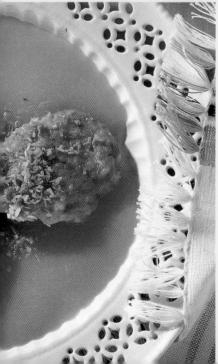

SPICED PEAR AND BLUEBERRY PARCELS

This combination makes a delicious dessert for a summer's evening and can be cooked on an outdoor grill or in the oven.

INGREDIENTS

4 firm, ripe pears
2 tablespoons lemon juice
1 tablespoon low-fat spread, melted
1¼ cups blueberries
¼ cup light brown sugar
freshly ground black pepper

SERVES 4

NUTRITIONAL NOTES

Per portion:

Calories	146
Fat, total	1.8g
Saturated fat	0.37g
Cholesterol	0.2mg
Fiber	4g

2 Cut four squares of heavy-duty foil, each large enough to wrap a pear, and brush with melted spread. Place two pear halves on each, cut side upward. Gather the foil around them, to hold them level.

3 Mix the blueberries and sugar together and spoon them on top of the pears. Sprinkle with black pepper. Wrap the foil over and cook for 20–25 minutes on a fairly hot grill or in the oven.

1 Prepare the grill or preheat the oven to 400°F. Peel the pears thinly. Cut in half lengthwise. Scoop out the core from each half. Brush the pears with lemon juice, to stop them from browning.

COOK'S TIP

To assemble the dessert in advance, place greaseproof baking parchment inside the parcel, because the acid in the lemon juice may react with the foil and taint the flavor.

FRUIT AND SPICE BREAD PUDDING

An easy-to-make fruity dessert with a hint of spice, this is delicious served
either hot or cold.

2 Mix together the raisins, apricots, sugar
and spice and sprinkle half the fruit
mixture over the bread in the dish.

3 Top with the remaining bread triangles
and then sprinkle over the remaining fruit.

4 Beat the eggs, milk and lemon zest
together and pour over the bread. Set
aside for about 30 minutes, to allow the
bread to absorb some of the liquid. Bake
for 45–60 minutes, until lightly set and
golden brown. Serve hot or cold.

INGREDIENTS

6 medium slices whole-wheat bread
2 ounces apricot or strawberry jam
low-fat spread, for greasing
1/3 cup golden raisins
1/4 cup dried apricots, chopped
1/3 cup light brown sugar
1 teaspoon ground apple pie spice
2 eggs
2 1/2 cups skim milk
finely grated zest of 1 lemon

SERVES 4

1 Preheat the oven to 325°F. Remove
and discard the crusts from the bread.
Spread the bread slices with jam and
cut into small triangles. Place half the
bread triangles in a lightly greased
ovenproof dish.

NUTRITIONAL NOTES
Per portion:

Calories	305
Fat, total	4.51g
Saturated fat	1.27g
Cholesterol	99.3mg
Fiber	3.75g

FRUITY BREAD PUDDING

A delicious family favorite from grandmother's kitchen, with a lighter, healthier
touch for today.

NUTRITIONAL NOTES

Per portion:

Calories	190
Fat, total	0.89g
Saturated fat	0.21g
Cholesterol	0.75mg
Fiber	1.8g

2 Remove the pan from the heat and stir
in the bread cubes, spice and banana.
Spoon the mixture into a shallow 5-cup
ovenproof dish and pour the milk over.

3 Sprinkle with demerara sugar and bake
for 25–30 minutes, until firm and golden
brown. Serve hot or cold, with plain
yogurt if you like.

INGREDIENTS

1/2 cup mixed dried fruit
2/3 cup unsweetened apple juice
3–4 slices day-old whole wheat
or white bread, cubed
1 teaspoon apple pie spice
1 large banana, sliced
2/3 cup skim milk
1 tablespoon demerara sugar
low-fat plain yogurt, to serve (optional)

SERVES 4

1 Preheat the oven to 400°F. Place the
dried fruit in a small pan with the apple
juice and bring to a boil.

BAKED APPLES WITH RED WINE

—

Special-occasion baked apples include a delicious filling of golden raisins soaked in spiced red wine.

INGREDIENTS

scant ¹/₂ cup golden raisins
1¹/₂ cups red wine
pinch of grated nutmeg
pinch of ground cinnamon
¹/₄ cup granulated sugar
pinch of grated lemon zest
7 teaspoons low-fat spread
6 baking apples of even size

SERVES 6

1 Put the golden raisins in a small bowl and pour the wine over. Stir in the grated nutmeg, ground cinnamon, sugar and lemon zest. Cover and let stand for approximately 1 hour.

2 Preheat the oven to 375°F. Use a little of the low-fat spread to grease a baking dish. Core the apples, without cutting right through to the bottom.

3 Divide the raisin mixture among the apples. Spoon in a little extra spiced wine. Arrange the apples in the prepared baking dish.

4 Pour the remaining wine around the apples. Top the filling in each apple with 1 teaspoon of the remaining spread. Bake for 40–50 minutes, or until the apples are soft but not mushy. Serve hot or at room temperature.

NUTRITIONAL NOTES

Per portion:

Calories	187Kcals
Fat, total	2.7g
Saturated fat	0.61g
Cholesterol	0.4mg
Fiber	2.6g

BAKED APPLES WITH APRICOT-NUT FILLING

—

This is an interesting version of an old favorite. Omit the low-fat spread if you
want to reduce the fat content further.

INGREDIENTS

1/2 cup chopped dried apricots

3 tablespoons chopped walnuts

1 teaspoon grated lemon zest

1/4 teaspoon ground cinnamon

2/3 cup light brown sugar

2 tablespoons low-fat spread

6 Golden Delicious or other cooking apples

SERVES 6

3 Stand the apples in a baking dish just large enough to hold them comfortably side by side.

4 Melt the remaining low-fat spread and brush it over the apples. Bake for 40–45 minutes or until tender. Serve hot.

1 Preheat the oven to 375°F. In a bowl, combine the apricots, walnuts, lemon zest and cinnamon. Add the sugar and rub in two-thirds of the low-fat spread until thoroughly combined.

2 Core the apples, without cutting all the way through to the bottom. Peel the top third of each apple. With a small knife, widen the top of each cavity by about 1½ inches for the filling. Spoon the filling into the apples.

NUTRITIONAL NOTES

Per portion:

Calories	263
Fat, total	4.9g
Saturated fat	0.89g
Cholesterol	0.3mg
Fiber	4.3g

BAKED APPLES IN HONEY AND LEMON

A classic combination of flavors in a healthy, traditional family dessert.
Serve warm, with skim-milk custard, if you like.

2 With a channel knife or a sharp knife with a narrow pointed blade, cut lines through the apple skin at intervals. Stand the apples in an ovenproof dish.

3 Mix together the honey, lemon zest, juice and low-fat spread.

INGREDIENTS

4 cooking apples
1 tablespoon honey
grated zest and juice of 1 lemon
1 tablespoon low-fat spread
skim-milk custard, to serve (optional)

SERVES 4

NUTRITIONAL NOTES

Per portion:

Calories	78
Fat, total	1.7g
Saturated fat	0.37g
Cholesterol	0.2mg
Fiber	2.4g

1 Preheat the oven to 350°F. Remove the cores from the apples, taking care not to go right through the bottoms of the apples.

4 Spoon the mixture into the apples and cover the dish with foil or a lid. Bake for 40–45 minutes, or until the apples are tender. Serve with skim-milk custard, if you like.

DATE, CHOCOLATE AND WALNUT PUDDING

—

Proper puddings are not totally taboo when you're reducing your fat intake—
this one is just within the rules!

2 Separate the whole egg and place the yolk in a heatproof bowl. Add the vanilla extract and sugar. Place the bowl over a pan of hot water and beat to thicken.

3 Sift the flour and cocoa into the mixture and fold in. Stir in the milk. Beat the egg whites and fold them in.

4 Spoon the mixture into the bowl and bake for 40–45 minutes, or until the pudding has risen well and is firm to the touch. Run a knife around the pudding then turn it out and serve immediately.

INGREDIENTS

low-fat spread, for greasing
1 tablespoon chopped walnuts
2 tablespoons chopped dates
1 egg plus 1 egg white
1 teaspoon pure vanilla extract
2 tablespoons demerara sugar
3 tablespoons whole-wheat flour
1 tablespoon cocoa powder
2 tablespoons skim milk

SERVES 4

1 Preheat the oven to 350°F. Grease a 5-cup pudding bowl and place a small circle of waxed paper or baking parchment in the bottom. Spoon in the walnuts and dates.

NUTRITIONAL NOTES

Per portion:

Calories	126
Fat, total	4.9g
Saturated fat	1.15g
Cholesterol	48.3mg
Fiber	1.3g

GOLDEN RAISIN AND COUSCOUS PUDDINGS

Most couscous on the market is the pre-cooked variety, which hardly needs cooking, but check the package instructions first. Serve hot, with skim-milk custard, if you like.

INGREDIENTS

1/3 cup golden raisins
2 cups unsweetened
apple juice
scant 1 cup couscous
1/2 teaspoon apple pie spice
skim-milk custard, to serve (optional)

SERVES 4

NUTRITIONAL NOTES

Per portion:

Calories	132
Fat, total	0.4g
Saturated fat	0.09g
Cholesterol	0mg
Fiber	0.3g

1 Lightly grease four 1-cup pudding bowls. Place the golden raisins and apple juice in a pan.

2 Bring the apple juice to a boil, then lower the heat and simmer the mixture gently for 2–3 minutes, to plump up the fruit. Lift out about half the fruit and place it in the bottom of the bowls.

3 Add the couscous and apple pie spice to the pan and bring the liquid back to a boil, stirring. Cover and cook over low heat for 8–10 minutes, or until all the liquid has been absorbed.

4 Spoon the couscous into the bowls, spread it level, then cover the bowls tightly with foil. Place the bowls in a steamer over boiling water, cover and steam for about 30 minutes. Run a knife around the edges, turn the puddings out carefully and serve immediately, with skim-milk custard, if you like.

COOK'S TIP

If you prefer, these puddings can be cooked in the microwave instead of steaming. Use individual microwave-safe bowls or teacups, cover them and microwave on high for 8–10 minutes.

BLACKBERRY COBBLER

—

Cobblers are easy to make and delicious to eat. This one has a juicy
blackberry compote under a biscuit blanket.

INGREDIENTS

7 cups blackberries
generous 1 cup granulated sugar
3 tablespoons all-purpose flour
grated zest of 1 lemon
1/4 teaspoon grated nutmeg

FOR THE TOPPING

2 cups all-purpose flour
1 cup granulated sugar
1 tablespoon baking powder
pinch of salt
1 cup skim milk
6 tablespoons low-fat spread, melted

SERVES 8

1 Preheat the oven to 350°F. In a large
mixing bowl, combine the blackberries
with 1 cup of the sugar. Add the flour
and lemon zest. Using a large spoon,
stir gently to blend. Transfer to a
8-cup baking dish.

2 Make the topping. Sift the flour, sugar,
baking powder and salt into a large bowl.
Set aside. In a bowl, combine the milk
and melted low-fat spread.

3 Gradually stir the milk mixture into
the dry ingredients and stir until the
batter is smooth.

4 Spoon the batter over the berries. Mix
the remaining sugar with the nutmeg,
then sprinkle the mixture over the batter.
Bake for about 50 minutes, until the
topping is set. Serve hot.

NUTRITIONAL NOTES

Per portion:

Calories	427
Fat, total	4.5g
Saturated fat	1g
Cholesterol	1.2mg
Fiber	4.1g

PEACH COBBLER

—

**All the flavor of the traditional and popular dessert,
with less fat than in a conventional cobbler.**

INGREDIENTS

5 cups peaches, peeled and sliced
3 tablespoons sugar
2 tablespoons peach brandy
1 tablespoon fresh lemon juice
1 tablespoon cornstarch

FOR THE TOPPING

1 cup all-purpose flour
1 1/2 teaspoons baking powder
1/4 teaspoon salt
1/4 cup ground almonds
2 1/2 ounces sugar
2 tablespoons low-fat spread
5 tablespoons skim milk
1/4 teaspoon almond extract
ice cream, to serve (optional)

SERVES 6

1 Preheat the oven to 425°F. In a bowl, toss the peaches with the sugar, peach brandy, lemon juice and cornstarch. Spoon the peach mixture into a 2-quart baking dish.

2 Make the topping. Using a fine sieve, sift the flour, baking powder and salt into a mixing bowl. Stir in the ground almonds and 2 ounces of the sugar. With 2 knives, or a pastry blender, cut in the spread until the mixture resembles coarse crumbs.

3 Add the milk and almond extract and stir until the mixture is just combined.

4 Drop the almond mixture on to the peaches. Sprinkle with the remaining sugar.

5 Bake for 30–35 minutes until piping hot. The cobbler topping should be lightly browned. Serve hot, with low-fat frozen yogurt, if you like.

NUTRITIONAL NOTES
Per portion:

Calories	393
Fat, total	4.4g
Saturated fat	0.68g
Cholesterol	0.6mg
Fiber	4g

APPLE BROWN BETTY

—

A traditional favorite, this tasty dessert is good with low-fat yogurt
or fromage frais.

INGREDIENTS
1 cup fresh white bread crumbs
low-fat spread, for greasing
1 cup light brown sugar
1/2 teaspoon ground cinnamon
1/4 teaspoon ground cloves
1/4 teaspoon grated nutmeg
2 pounds apples
juice of 1 lemon
2 tablespoons low-fat spread
3 tablespoons finely chopped walnuts

SERVES 6

1 Preheat the grill. Spread the bread crumbs on a baking sheet and toast under the broiler until golden, stirring so that they color evenly. Set aside.

2 Preheat the oven to 375°F. Grease a 8-cup baking dish. Mix the sugar with the ground cinnamon, cloves and grated nutmeg in a medium-sized mixing bowl.

3 Peel, core and slice the apples. Toss the apple slices with the lemon juice to prevent them from turning brown.

4 Sprinkle about 3 tablespoons of the bread crumbs over the bottom of the prepared dish. Cover with one-third of the apples and sprinkle one-third of the sugar-spice mixture on top.

5 Add another layer of bread crumbs and dot with one-quarter of the spread. Repeat the layers two more times, ending with a layer of bread crumbs. Sprinkle with the nuts, and dot with the remaining spread.

6 Bake for 35–40 minutes, until the apples are tender and the top is golden brown. Serve warm.

NUTRITIONAL NOTES
Per portion:

Calories	257
Fat, total	4.7g
Saturated fat	0.73g
Cholesterol	0.3mg
Fiber	2.9g

BLUEBERRY BUCKLE

—

**This fruity dessert is an American speciality and can be served with
low-fat plain yogurt, if you like.**

INGREDIENTS
low-fat spread, for greasing
2 cups all-purpose flour
2 teaspoons baking powder
1/2 teaspoon salt
2 tablespoons low-fat spread
3/4 cup granulated sugar
1 egg
1/2 teaspoon pure vanilla extract
3/4 cup skim milk
4 cups fresh blueberries
low-fat plain yogurt, to serve (optional)

FOR THE TOPPING
2/3 cup light brown sugar
1/2 cup all-purpose flour
1/2 teaspoon salt
1/2 teaspoon ground allspice
3 tablespoons low-fat spread
2 teaspoons skim milk
1 teaspoon pure vanilla extract

SERVES 8

1 Preheat the oven to 375°F. Grease a 9-inch round gratin dish or shallow baking dish. Sift the flour, baking powder and salt into a bowl. Set aside.

2 Cream the low-fat spread and the sugar. Beat in the egg and vanilla extract. Add the flour mixture alternately with the milk, beginning and ending with flour.

3 Pour the mixture into the prepared dish and sprinkle the blueberries over.

4 Make the topping. Mix the brown sugar, flour, salt and allspice in a bowl. Rub in the spread until the mixture resembles coarse crumbs.

NUTRITIONAL NOTES
Per portion:

Calories	338
Fat, total	4.9g
Saturated fat	1.14g
Cholesterol	25.1mg
Fiber	2.1g

5 Mix the milk and vanilla extract together. Drizzle over the flour mixture and mix with a fork. Sprinkle the topping over the blueberries. Bake for 45 minutes, or until a skewer inserted in the center comes out clean. Serve warm, with low-fat plain yogurt, if you like.

APPLE AND WALNUT CRUMBLE

—

Another American favorite, combining delicious apples with crunchy walnuts
for a simple, but tasty, dessert.

INGREDIENTS

low-fat spread, for greasing
2 pounds apples, peeled and sliced
grated zest of 1/2 lemon
1 tablespoon fresh lemon juice
1/2 cup light brown sugar
3/4 cup all-purpose flour
1/4 teaspoon salt
1/4 teaspoon grated nutmeg
1/2 teaspoon ground cardamom
1/2 teaspoon ground cinnamon
2 tablespoons low-fat spread
3 tablespoons walnut pieces, chopped

SERVES 6

1 Preheat the oven to 350°F. Grease a
9-inch oval gratin dish or shallow baking
dish. Toss the apples with the lemon zest
and juice. Arrange them evenly in the
bottom of the prepared dish.

2 In a mixing bowl, combine the brown
sugar, flour, salt, nutmeg, cardamom and
cinnamon. Rub in the spread until the
mixture resembles coarse crumbs. Mix in
the walnuts.

3 With a spoon, sprinkle the walnut and
spice mixture evenly over the apples.
Cover with foil and bake for 30 minutes.

4 Remove the foil and continue baking
for about 30 minutes more, until the
apples are tender and the crumble
topping is crisp. Serve warm.

NUTRITIONAL NOTES

Per portion:

Calories	240
Fat, total	4.7g
Saturated fat	0.76g
Cholesterol	0.3mg
Fiber	3.1g

STRAWBERRY AND APPLE CRUMBLE

A high-fiber, low-fat version of the classic apple crumble. Fresh or frozen raspberries
can be used instead of strawberries.

2 Toss together the apples, strawberries, sugar, cinnamon and orange juice. Place the mixture into a 5-cup ovenproof dish.

3 Make the crumble. Combine the flour and oats in a bowl and mix in the low-fat spread with a fork.

4 Sprinkle the crumble evenly over the fruit. Bake for 40–45 minutes, until golden brown and bubbling. Serve warm, with low-fat custard or yogurt, if you like.

INGREDIENTS

1 pound cooking apples
1¹/4 cups strawberries, hulled
2 tablespoons sugar
¹/2 teaspoon ground cinnamon
2 tablespoons orange juice
low-fat custard or yogurt, to serve (optional)

FOR THE CRUMBLE

3 tablespoons plain whole-wheat flour
2/3 cup rolled oats
2 tablespoons low-fat spread

SERVES 4

1 Preheat the oven to 350°F. Peel, core and cut the apples into approximately ¹/4-inch slices. Halve the strawberries.

NUTRITIONAL NOTES
Per portion:

Calories	173
Fat, total	3.9g
Saturated fat	0.85g
Cholesterol	0.4mg
Fiber	3.5g

BLACKBERRY CHARLOTTE

A classic dessert, the perfect reward for an afternoon's
blackberry picking.

INGREDIENTS

2 tablespoons low-fat spread
3 cups fresh white bread crumbs
1/3 cup light brown sugar
1/4 cup light corn syrup
finely grated zest and juice of 2 lemons
1 pound cooking apples
4 cups blackberries

NUTRITIONAL NOTES

Per portion:

Calories	346
Fat, total	4.2g
Saturated fat	0.74g
Cholesterol	0.5mg
Fiber	6.3g

SERVES 4

1 Preheat the oven to 350°F. Melt the
spread in a pan with the bread crumbs.
Sauté for 5–7 minutes, until the crumbs
are golden and fairly crisp. Let
cool slightly.

2 Heat the sugar, syrup, lemon zest and
juice gently in a small saucepan. Add the
crumbs and mix well.

3 With a sharp knife, cut the apples into
quarters, peel them and remove the cores.
Slice the wedges thinly.

4 Arrange a thin layer of blackberries in
a baking dish. Top with a thin layer of
crumbs, then a thin layer of apple,
topping the fruit with another thin layer of
crumbs. Repeat the process with another
layer of blackberries, followed by a layer
of crumbs.

5 Continue until you have used up all
the ingredients, finishing with a layer
of crumbs.

5 Bake for 30 minutes, until the crumbs
are golden and the fruit is soft.

COOK'S TIP
When layering the fruit and crumbs the
mixture should be piled well above the
top edge of the dish, because it shrinks
during cooking.

BAKED APPLE CHUNKS

—

This filling, economical family dessert is a good way of using up bread that is a day or so old.
The crunchy topping contrasts beautifully with the apples.

INGREDIENTS

1 pound cooking apples
3 ounces whole-wheat bread, about
3 slices, without crusts
1/2 cup low-fat cottage cheese
3 tablespoons light brown sugar
scant 1 cup skim milk
1 teaspoon demerara sugar

SERVES 4

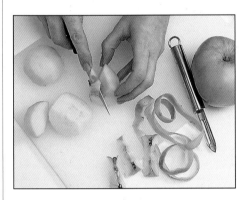

1 Preheat the oven to 425°F. Peel the apples, cut them into quarters and remove the cores.

2 Using a sharp knife, roughly chop the apples into even-sized pieces, about 1/2-inch in width and depth.

3 Cut the bread into 1/2-inch cubes. Do not use crusts as these will be too thick for the mixture.

4 Put the apples in a bowl and add the bread cubes, cottage cheese and brown sugar. Toss lightly to mix.

5 Stir in the skim milk and then pour the mixture into a wide ovenproof dish. Sprinkle demerara sugar over the top of the mixture.

6 Bake for 30–35 minutes, or until the apple bake is golden brown and bubbling. Serve hot.

VARIATIONS

You can experiment with other types of bread such as oat, rye or white. Pears can be used instead of apples.

NUTRITIONAL NOTES

Per portion:

Calories	158
Fat, total	1g
Saturated fat	0.38g
Cholesterol	2.4mg
Fiber	2.3g

COOK'S TIP

You may need to adjust the amount of milk used, depending on the dryness of the bread; the more stale the bread, the more milk it will absorb. The texture should be very moist but not falling apart.

APPLE COUSCOUS PUDDING

This unusual mixture makes a delicious family dessert with a rich fruity
flavor, but virtually no fat.

INGREDIENTS

*2¹/₂ cups unsweetened
apple juice*
²/₃ cup couscous
¹/₄ cup golden raisins
¹/₂ teaspoon apple pie spice
2 large cooking apples
2 tablespoons demerara sugar
low-fat plain yogurt, to serve

SERVES 4

NUTRITIONAL NOTES

Per portion:

Calories	194
Fat, total	0.58g
Saturated fat	0.09g
Cholesterol	0mg
Fiber	0.75g

1 Preheat the oven to 400°F. Bring to boil
the apple juice, couscous, golden raisins
and spice in a pan, stirring. Lower heat,
cover and simmer.

COOK'S TIP

Couscous is a pre-cooked pasta that is
widely available in supermarkets and
health food shops.

2 Spoon half the couscous mixture into
a 5-cup ovenproof dish. Peel, core and
slice the apples and arrange half the
slices over the couscous. Top with the
remaining couscous.

3 Arrange the remaining apple slices
over the top and sprinkle with demerara
sugar. Bake for 25–30 minutes, or until
golden brown. Serve while still hot, with
low-fat yogurt.

BAKED FRUIT COMPOTE

—

**This marvelous medley of dried fruit looks good, tastes even better
and is quick and easy to make.**

INGREDIENTS

2/3 cup dried figs

1/2 cup dried apricots

1/2 cup dried apple rings

1/4 cup prunes

1/2 cup dried pears

1/2 cup dried peaches

1 1/4 cups unsweetened apple juice

1 1/4 cups orange juice

6 cloves

1 cinnamon stick

a few toasted flaked almonds, to decorate

SERVES 6

2 Mix together the unsweetened apple and orange juices and pour evenly over the fruit. Add the cloves and cinnamon stick and stir gently to mix. Make sure that all the fruit has been thoroughly coated with the apple and orange juices.

3 Bake for about 30 minutes until the fruit mixture is hot, stirring once or twice during cooking. Set aside and let soak for 20 minutes, then remove and discard the cloves and cinnamon stick.

4 Spoon into serving bowls and serve warm or cold, decorated with toasted flaked almonds.

COOK'S TIP
Use other mixtures of unsweetened fruit juices, such as pineapple and orange or grape and apple.

1 Preheat the oven to 350°F. Place the figs, apricots, apple rings, prunes, pears and peaches in a shallow ovenproof dish and stir to mix.

NUTRITIONAL NOTES
Per portion:

Calories	174
Fat, total	0.8g
Saturated fat	0.05g
Cholesterol	0mg
Fiber	5.16g

KUMQUAT COMPOTE

Warm, spicy and full of sun-ripened ingredients—this is the perfect winter dessert
to remind you of long summer days.

2 Pare the orange zest and add to the pan.
Peel and grate the ginger and add to the
pan. Crush the cardamom pods and add
the seeds to the mixture, with the cloves.

3 Reduce the heat, cover the pan
and let simmer gently for about
30 minutes, or until the fruit is tender,
stirring occasionally.

4 Add the squeezed orange juice to the
compote. Sweeten with the honey,
sprinkle with the almonds and serve warm.

INGREDIENTS

2 cups kumquats

scant 1 cup dried apricots

2 tablespoons golden raisins

1²/3 cups water

1 orange

1-inch piece of fresh ginger root

4 cardamom pods

4 cloves

2 tablespoons honey

1 tablespoon flaked almonds, toasted

SERVES 4

1 Wash the kumquats, and, if they are
large, cut them in half. Place them in a
pan with the apricots, golden raisins and
water. Bring to a boil.

NUTRITIONAL NOTES
Per portion:

Calories	198
Fat, total	2.9g
Saturated fat	0.25g
Cholesterol	0mg
Fiber	6.9g

RUSSIAN CURRANT PUDDING

This fruit compote from Russia, called Kissel, is traditionally made from the thickened juice of
stewed red or black currants. This recipe uses the whole fruit with added blackberry liqueur.

INGREDIENTS

2 cups red or black currants or
a mixture of both
2 cups raspberries
2/3 cup water
1/4 cup sugar
1 1/2 tablespoons arrowroot
1 tablespoon crème de mûre
low-fat plain yogurt, to serve (optional)

SERVES 4

1 Place the currants and raspberries,
water and sugar in a pan. Cover the
pan and cook over low heat for
12–15 minutes, until the fruit is soft.

2 Blend the arrowroot to a paste with a
little water in a small bowl and stir into
the hot fruit mixture. Bring the fruit
mixture back to a boil, stirring all the
time until thickened and smooth.

3 Remove the pan from the heat and
allow the fruit compote to cool slightly,
then gently stir in the crème de mûre.

4 Pour the compote into four glass
serving bowls and set aside until cold,
then chill until required. Serve alone or
with spoonfuls of low-fat plain yogurt.

NUTRITIONAL NOTES
Per portion:

Calories	105
Fat, total	0.2g
Saturated fat	0g
Cholesterol	0mg
Fiber	3.3g

COOK'S TIP
Crème de mûre is a blackberry liqueur
available from large supermarkets—
you could use crème de cassis instead,
if you prefer.

CORNFLAKE-TOPPED BAKED PEACHES

With just a few pantry ingredients, this golden, crisp-crusted, family
dessert can be prepared in next to no time.

INGREDIENTS

1 can (14¹/₂ ounces) peach slices in juice
2 tablespoons golden raisins
1 cinnamon stick
strip of pared orange zest
2 tablespoons low-fat spread
1¹/₂ cups cornflakes
2 teaspoons sesame seeds

SERVES 4

1 Preheat the oven to 400°F. Drain the
peaches, reserving the juice in a small
saucepan. Arrange the peach slices in a
shallow ovenproof dish.

2 Add the golden raisins, cinnamon stick
and orange zest to the juice and bring to a
boil. Lower the heat and simmer, for
3–4 minutes, to reduce the liquid by half.
Remove the cinnamon stick and zest and
spoon the syrup over the peaches.

3 Melt the low-fat spread in a small pan,
stir in the cornflakes and sesame seeds.

4 Spread the cornflake mixture over the
fruit. Bake for 15–20 minutes, or until the
topping is crisp and golden. Serve hot.

NUTRITIONAL NOTES
Per portion:

Calories	150
Fat, total	4.6g
Saturated fat	1g
Cholesterol	0.5mg
Fiber	1.3g

RHUBARB SPIRAL COBBLER

The tangy taste of rhubarb combines perfectly with the ginger spice
in this unusual jelly roll.

3 Roll out the dough on a floured surface
to a 10-inch square. Mix the orange zest,
demerara sugar and ginger, then sprinkle
this over the dough.

4 Roll up quite tightly, then cut into
about 10 slices using a sharp knife.
Arrange the slices over the rhubarb.

5 Bake for 20–25 minutes, or until the
spirals are well risen and golden brown.
Serve warm.

INGREDIENTS

1¹/2 pounds rhubarb, sliced
3 tablespoons unsweetened orange juice
6 tablespoons sugar
1³/4 cups self-rising flour
1 cup low-fat plain yogurt
grated zest of 1 orange
2 tablespoons demerara sugar
1 teaspoon ground ginger

SERVES 4

1 Preheat the oven to 400°F. Mix the
rhubarb, orange juice and 4 tablespoons
of the sugar in a pan. Cover and cook over
low heat for 10 minutes or until tender.
Pour into an ovenproof dish.

NUTRITIONAL NOTES

Per portion:

Calories	320
Fat, total	1.2g
Saturated fat	0.34g
Cholesterol	2mg
Fiber	3.92g

2 To make the topping, mix the flour
and remaining sugar in a bowl, then
stir in enough of the yogurt to bind to a
soft dough.

COOK'S TIP

In the summer you can substitute
halved plums, sliced nectarines or
peaches for the rhubarb, if you prefer.

PLUM, APPLE AND BANANA SCONE PIE

This is one of those simple, satisfying desserts that everyone enjoys. It is delicious hot or cold
and can be served on its own or with low-fat plain yogurt.

INGREDIENTS

1 pound plums
1 cooking apple
1 large banana
2/3 cup water
1 cup whole-wheat flour, or half
whole-wheat and half all-purpose flour
2 teaspoons baking powder
3 tablespoons raisins
1/4 cup sour milk or
low-fat plain yogurt
low-fat plain yogurt, to serve (optional)

SERVES 4

1 Preheat the oven to 350°F. Cut the plums in half and ease out the pits. Peel, core and chop the apple, then slice the banana.

NUTRITIONAL NOTES

Per portion:

Calories	195
Fat, total	1g
Saturated fat	0.2g
Cholesterol	0.6mg
Fiber	5.2g

2 Mix the fruit in a saucepan. Pour in the water. Bring to simmering point and cook gently for 15 minutes, or until the fruit is completely soft.

3 Spoon the fruit mixture into a pie dish. Level the surface.

4 Mix the flour, baking powder and raisins in a bowl. Add the sour milk or low-fat plain yogurt and mix to a very soft dough.

5 Transfer the scone dough to a lightly floured surface and divide it into 6–8 portions, then pat them into flattish scones.

6 Cover the plum and apple mixture with the scones. Bake the pie for 40 minutes until the scone topping is cooked through. Serve the pie hot with plain yogurt, or set aside until cold.

COOK'S TIP

To prevent the banana discoloring before cooking, dip each slice in fresh lemon juice.

GRIDDLE CAKES WITH MULLED PLUMS

—

These wonderfully light little pancakes, with their rich, spicy plum sauce, are designed to be
cooked on an outdoor grill, but can just as easily be cooked on the stove.

INGREDIENTS

1¼ pounds red plums
6 tablespoons light brown sugar
1 cinnamon stick
2 whole cloves
1 piece star anise
6 tablespoons unsweetened apple juice
low-fat plain yogurt or fromage frais,
to serve (optional)

FOR THE GRIDDLE CAKES

½ cup all-purpose flour
2 teaspoons baking powder
pinch of salt
½ cup fine cornmeal
2 tablespoons light brown sugar
1 egg, beaten
1¼ cups skim milk
1 tablespoon corn oil

SERVES 6

1 Halve, pit and quarter the plums. Place
them in a pan, with the sugar, spices and
apple juice.

COOK'S TIP

Use spray oil on the griddle if you
prefer, and cut the fat content
still further.

2 Place on a hot grill or burner and bring
to a boil. Lower heat, cover and simmer
gently for 8–10 minutes, stirring, until the
plums are soft. Remove the spices and
keep the plums warm.

3 For the griddle cakes, sift the flour,
baking powder and salt into a large bowl
and stir in the cornmeal and sugar.

4 Make a well in the center and add the
egg; gradually beat in the milk. Beat with
a whisk or wooden spoon to form a smooth
batter. Beat in 1 teaspoon of the oil.

5 Heat a griddle or a heavy frying pan on
a hot grill or burner. When it is very hot,
brush it with some of the remaining oil
and then drop tablespoons of batter onto
it. Cook the griddle cakes for about a
minute, until bubbles start to appear on
the surface and the underside is golden.

6 Turn the cakes over and cook the other
side for another minute, or until golden.
Bake the other cakes. Serve hot with the
mulled plums. Add a spoonful of low-fat
plain yogurt or fromage frais, if you like.

NUTRITIONAL NOTES
Per portion:

Calories	159
Fat, total	3.3g
Saturated fat	0.58g
Cholesterol	33.1mg
Fiber	1.7g

GRILLED BANANAS WITH SPICY VANILLA SPREAD

Baked bananas are a must for the outdoor grill—they're so easy because they cook
in their own skins and need no preparation at all.

2 Meanwhile, split the cardamom pods
and remove the seeds. Place the seeds in
a mortar and crush lightly with a pestle.

3 Split the vanilla bean lengthwise and
scrape out the tiny seeds. Mix with the
cardamom seeds, orange zest, brandy,
sugar and spread, to make a thick paste.

4 Slit the skin of each banana, open out
slightly and spoon in a little of the paste.
Serve immediately.

INGREDIENTS

4 bananas
6 green cardamom pods
1 vanilla bean
finely grated zest of 1 small orange
2 tablespoons brandy
1/4 cup light brown sugar
3 tablespoons low-fat spread

SERVES 4

1 Place the bananas, in their skins, on
the hot grill and leave for 6–8 minutes,
turning occasionally, until they are
turning brownish black.

COOK'S TIP

If making this for children, use orange
juice instead of the brandy or, if the fat
content is no object, drizzle the cooked
bananas with melted chocolate.

NUTRITIONAL NOTES
Per portion:

Calories	215
Fat, total	4.9g
Saturated fat	1.22g
Cholesterol	0.7mg
Fiber	1.1g

HOT SPICED BANANAS

—

**Baking bananas in a rum and fruit syrup makes for a dessert with negligible
fat and maximum flavor.**

INGREDIENTS

low-fat spread, for greasing
6 ripe bananas
generous 1 cup light brown sugar
1 cup unsweetened
pineapple juice
¹⁄2 cup dark rum
2 cinnamon sticks
12 whole cloves

SERVES 6

NUTRITIONAL NOTES

Per portion:

Calories	290
Fat, total	0.3g
Saturated fat	0.11g
Cholesterol	0mg
Fiber	1.1g

3 Mix the sugar and pineapple juice in a saucepan. Heat gently until the sugar has dissolved, stirring occasionally. Add the rum, cinnamon sticks and cloves. Bring to a boil, then remove the pan from heat.

4 Pour the hot pineapple and spice mixture over the bananas in the baking dish. Bake in the oven for approximately 25–30 minutes, until the bananas are hot and very tender. Serve while still hot.

1 Preheat the oven to 350°F. Grease a 9-inch baking dish.

2 Peel the bananas and cut them diagonally into 1-inch pieces. Arrange the banana pieces evenly over the bottom of the prepared baking dish.

RUM AND RAISIN BANANAS

—

**Choose almost-ripe bananas with evenly colored skins, either all yellow
or just green at the tips.**

INGREDIENTS
¹/4 cup raisins
5 tablespoons dark rum
1 tablespoon low-fat spread
¹/4 cup light brown sugar
*4 ripe bananas, peeled and
halved lengthwise*
¹/4 teaspoon grated nutmeg
¹/4 teaspoon ground cinnamon
1 tablespoon slivered almonds, toasted
*low-fat fromage frais or low-fat vanilla
ice cream, to serve (optional)*

SERVES 4

1 Put the raisins in a bowl and pour the
rum over. Let them soak for about
30 minutes, until plump.

2 Melt the spread in a frying pan,
add the sugar and stir until it has
completely dissolved. Add the bananas
and cook for a few minutes until tender,
turning occasionally.

3 Sprinkle the spices over the bananas,
then pour the rum and raisins over.
Carefully set alight using a long-handled
match; stir gently to mix.

4 Scatter the slivered almonds over and
serve immediately with low-fat fromage
frais or low-fat vanilla ice cream, if you like.

COOK'S TIP
For an accompaniment that won't add
too much to the fat content of this
dessert, make your own yogurt freeze
by churning low-fat yogurt in an ice-
cream maker.

NUTRITIONAL NOTES
Per portion:

Calories	263
Fat, total	4.1g
Saturated fat	0.51g
Cholesterol	0.2mg
Fiber	1.6g

CARIBBEAN BANANAS

Tender baked bananas in a rich and spicy sauce of ground allspice and ginger—
a dessert for those with a sweet tooth!

INGREDIENTS

2 tablespoons low-fat spread
8 firm ripe bananas
juice of 1 lime
1/2 cup dark brown sugar
1 teaspoon ground allspice
1/2 teaspoon ground ginger
seeds from 6 cardamom pods, crushed
2 tablespoons rum
pared lime zest, to decorate
low-fat crème fraîche, to serve (optional)

SERVES 4

1 Preheat the oven to 400°F. Use a little of the spread to grease a shallow baking dish large enough to hold the bananas snugly in a single layer.

2 Peel the bananas and cut them in half lengthwise. Arrange the bananas in the dish and pour the lime juice over.

NUTRITIONAL NOTES

Per portion:

Calories	310
Fat, total	3.2g
Saturated fat	0.87g
Cholesterol	0.4mg
Fiber	2.2g

3 Mix the sugar, allspice, ginger and crushed cardamom seeds in a bowl. Scatter the mixture over the bananas. Dot with the remaining low-fat spread. Bake, basting once, for 15 minutes, or until the bananas are soft.

4 Remove the dish from the oven. Warm the rum in a small pan or metal soup ladle, pour it over the bananas and set it alight.

5 As soon as the flames die down, decorate the dessert with the pared lime zest. Serve while still hot and add a dollop of low-fat crème fraîche to each portion, if you like.

VARIATION

For a version that will appeal more to children, use orange juice instead of lime and leave out the rum.

GRILLED PINEAPPLE BOATS WITH RUM GLAZE

—

Fresh pineapple is even more full of flavor when broiled or grilled; this spiced rum glaze turns it
into a very special dessert.

INGREDIENTS
1 pineapple, about 1 pound 6 ounces
2 tablespoons dark brown sugar
1 teaspoon ground ginger
3 tablespoons low-fat spread, melted
2 tablespoons dark rum

SERVES 4

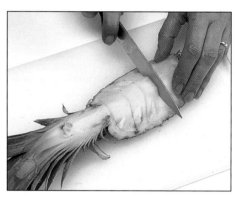

COOK'S TIP
For an easier version, cut off the skin
and then slice the whole pineapple into
thick slices and cook as above.

1 With a large, sharp knife, cut the
pineapple lengthwise into four equal
wedges. Cut out and discard the hard center
core from each wedge. Take care when
handling the pineapple's rough outer skin.

2 Cut between the flesh and skin, to
release the flesh, but leave the skin in
place. Slice the flesh across, into chunks.

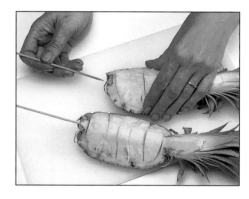

3 Push a bamboo skewer lengthwise
through each wedge and into the stalk,
to hold the chunks in place.

4 Mix together the sugar, ginger, melted
spread and rum and brush over the
pineapple. Cook the wedges on a hot grill
for 3–4 minutes; pour the remaining glaze
over the top and serve.

NUTRITIONAL NOTES
Per portion:

Calories	155
Fat, total	4.9g
Saturated fat	1.14g
Cholesterol	0.7mg
Fiber	1.8g

GRILLED NECTARINES WITH AMARETTO

Amaretto, the sweet almond-flavored liqueur from Italy, adds a touch of luxury
to these low-fat grilled nectarines.

INGREDIENTS

6 ripe nectarines

2 tablespoons honey

4 tablespoons Amaretto

reduced-fat crème fraîche,

to serve (optional)

SERVES 4

NUTRITIONAL NOTES

Per portion:

Calories	150
Fat, total	0.2g
Saturated fat	0g
Cholesterol	0mg
Fiber	2.7g

1 Cut the nectarines in half by running a small sharp knife down the side of each fruit from top to bottom, pushing the knife right through to the pit. Gently ease the nectarine apart and remove the pit. Handle the fruit carefully, because nectarines bruise easily.

2 Place the nectarines, cut side up, in an ovenproof dish and drizzle ½ teaspoon honey and 1 teaspoon Amaretto over each half. Preheat the broiler until very hot and then broil the fruit until slightly charred. Serve with a little reduced-fat crème fraîche, if you like.

NECTARINES WITH MARZIPAN AND YOGURT

—

A luscious dessert that few can resist; marzipan and nectarines are a
wonderful combination.

INGREDIENTS

4 firm, ripe nectarines or peaches
3 ounces marzipan
5 tablespoons low-fat plain yogurt
3 amaretti cookies, crushed

SERVES 4

1 Cut the nectarines or peaches in half,
removing the pits.

2 Cut the marzipan into eight pieces and
press one piece into the pit cavity of each
nectarine half. Preheat the broiler, unless
you are cooking on an outdoor grill.

COOK'S TIP

Either peaches or nectarines can
be used for this recipe. If the pit does
not pull out easily when you halve
the fruit, use a small, sharp knife
to cut around it.

3 Spoon the low-fat plain yogurt on top.
Sprinkle the crushed amaretti cookies
over the yogurt.

4 Place the fruits on a hot grill or under a
hot broiler. Cook for 3–5 minutes, until
the yogurt starts to melt.

NUTRITIONAL NOTES
Per portion:

Calories	176
Fat, total	4.3g
Saturated fat	0.98g
Cholesterol	3.2mg
Fiber	2.3g

SPICED NECTARINES WITH FROMAGE FRAIS

This easy dessert is good at any time of year—use canned peach halves if fresh
nectarines are not available.

2 Arrange the fruit, cut-side upwards,
in a wide flameproof dish or on a
baking sheet.

3 Stir the sugar into the fromage frais.
Using a teaspoon, spoon the mixture into
the hollow of each half.

4 Sprinkle the fruit with the ground star
anise. Place under a moderately hot
broiler for 6–8 minutes, or until the fruit
is hot and bubbling. Serve warm.

INGREDIENTS

4 ripe nectarines or peaches
1 tablespoon light brown sugar
1/2 cup low-fat fromage frais
1/2 teaspoon ground star anise

SERVES 4

1 With a sharp knife cut the nectarines
or peaches in half and remove the pits.

NUTRITIONAL NOTES

Per portion:

Calories	108
Fat, total	3.3g
Saturated fat	2g
Cholesterol	14.4mg
Fiber	1.5g

COOK'S TIP

If you can't get star anise, try ground
cloves or ground apple pie spice.

GRILLED ORANGE PARCELS

—

This is one of the most delicious ways of rounding off a party. The oranges are delicious on their own, but can be served with low-fat fromage frais, if you like.

INGREDIENTS

2 tablespoons low-fat spread, plus extra, melted, for brushing
4 oranges
2 tablespoons maple syrup
2 tablespoons Cointreau or Grand Marnier liqueur
low-fat fromage frais, to serve (optional)

SERVES 4

1 Cut four squares of heavy duty foil, large enough to wrap the oranges. Melt about 2 teaspoons of the low-fat spread and brush it over the center of each piece of foil.

2 Remove some shreds of orange zest, for the decoration. Blanch them, dry them and set them aside. Peel the oranges, removing all the white pith and peel and catching the juice in a bowl.

3 Slice the oranges crosswise into several thick slices. Reassemble them and place each orange on a square of foil.

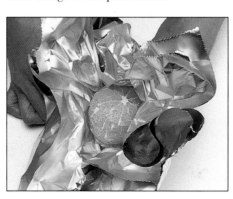

4 Create a cup shape by tucking the foil up high around the oranges. This will keep them in shape, but leave the foil open at the top.

5 Mix together the reserved orange juice, maple syrup and liqueur and spoon the mixture over the oranges.

6 Add a dab of low-fat spread to each parcel and fold over the foil, to seal in the juices. Place the parcels on a hot grill for 10–12 minutes, until hot. Serve topped with shreds of orange zest and fromage frais, if you like.

NUTRITIONAL NOTES
Per portion:

Calories	127
Fat, total	3.2g
Saturated fat	0.74g
Cholesterol	0.5mg
Fiber	2.7g

COOK'S TIP

To make the orange shreds for the decoration, slice off several pieces of orange zest, taking care to avoid the bitter white pith, then cut them into thin matchsticks. Add to a small pan of boiling water, for 1 minute, then drain and dry on paper towels.

APPLES AND RASPBERRIES IN ROSE SYRUP

Inspiration for this dessert stems from the fact that the apple and the raspberry belong to the
rose family. The subtle flavors are shared here in an infusion of rose-scented tea.

INGREDIENTS

1 teaspoon rose pouchong tea
3³/4 cups boiling water
1 teaspoon rosewater (optional)
¹/4 cup granulated sugar
1 teaspoon lemon juice
5 apples
1¹/2 cups fresh raspberries

SERVES 4

1 Warm a large tea pot. Add the rose
pouchong tea, then pour on the boiling
water, together with the rosewater, if
using. Let stand and infuse for
4 minutes.

2 Measure the sugar and lemon juice into
a stainless steel saucepan. Strain in the
tea and stir to dissolve the sugar.

3 Peel and core the apples, then cut
into quarters.

4 Poach the apples in the syrup for about
5 minutes.

5 Transfer the apples and syrup to
a large metal tray and let cool to
room temperature.

6 Pour the cooled apples and syrup into a
bowl, add the raspberries and mix to
combine. Spoon into individual dishes or
bowls and serve warm.

NUTRITIONAL NOTES
Per portion:

Calories	125
Fat, total	0.4g
Saturated fat	0g
Cholesterol	0mg
Fiber	3.6g

PAPAYA BAKED WITH GINGER

—

Ginger enhances the flavor of papaya in this recipe, which takes no more than
ten minutes to prepare.

INGREDIENTS

2 ripe papayas

2 pieces stem ginger in syrup, drained,
plus 1 tablespoon syrup from the jar

8 dessert cookies, coarsely crushed

3 tablespoons raisins

shredded, finely pared zest and juice
of 1 lime

1 tablespoon light brown sugar

¼ cup low-fat plain yogurt,
plus extra to serve (optional)

1 tablespoon finely chopped
unsalted pistachios

SERVES 4

COOK'S TIP

Don't overcook papaya or the flesh will
become very watery.

1 Preheat the oven to 400°F. Cut the
papayas in half and scoop out their
seeds. Place the halves in a baking dish
and set aside. Cut the stem ginger into
fine matchsticks.

2 Make the filling. Combine the crushed
cookies, stem ginger matchsticks and
raisins in a bowl. Make sure they are all
mixed well together.

3 Stir in the lime zest and juice, then add
the sugar and the yogurt. Mix well.

4 Fill the papaya halves and drizzle
with the ginger syrup. Sprinkle with
the pistachios.

5 Bake for about 25 minutes, or until
tender. Serve hot, with extra low-fat plain
yogurt, if you like.

NUTRITIONAL NOTES
Per portion:

Calories	218
Fat, total	4.2g
Saturated fat	1.23g
Cholesterol	6mg
Fiber	3.8g

BAKED PEACHES WITH RASPBERRY SAUCE

Pretty as a picture—that's the effect when you serve these tasty stuffed peaches
to delighted dinner party guests.

INGREDIENTS

2 tablespoons low-fat spread
1/4 cup granulated sugar
1 egg, beaten
1/4 cup ground almonds
6 ripe peaches
glossy leaves and plain or frosted
raspberries, to decorate

FOR THE SAUCE
2 cups raspberries
1 tablespoon confectioners' sugar

SERVES 6

NUTRITIONAL NOTES
Per portion:

Calories	137
Fat, total	4.7g
Saturated fat	0.81g
Cholesterol	32.3mg
Fiber	2.8g

1 Preheat the oven to 350°F. Beat
the low-fat spread and sugar together,
then beat in the egg and ground almonds.

2 Cut the peaches in half and remove the
pits. With a spoon, scrape out some of the
flesh from each peach half, slightly
enlarging the hollow left by the pit. Save
the excess peach flesh for the sauce.

3 Stand the peach halves on a baking
sheet, supporting them with crumpled foil
to keep them steady. Fill the hollow in
each peach half with the almond mixture.
Bake for 30 minutes, or until the almond
filling is puffed and golden and the
peaches are very tender.

4 Meanwhile, make the sauce. Combine
the raspberries and confectioners' sugar
in a food processor or blender. Add the
reserved peach flesh. Process until
smooth. Press through a strainer set over
a bowl to remove fibers and seeds.

5 Let the peaches cool slightly. Spoon the
sauce on each plate and arrange two peach
halves on top. Decorate with the leaves
and raspberries and serve immediately.

COOK'S TIP
For a special occasion, stir about
1 tablespoon framboise or peach
brandy into the raspberry sauce.

STUFFED PEACHES WITH ALMOND LIQUEUR

Together amaretti cookies and amaretto liqueur have an intense almond flavor,
and make a natural partner for peaches.

INGREDIENTS

4 ripe but firm peaches
1/2 cup amaretti cookies
2 tablespoons low-fat spread
2 tablespoons sugar
1 egg yolk
1/4 cup almond liqueur
low-fat spread, for greasing
1 cup dry white wine
8 tiny sprigs of fresh basil, to decorate
low-fat ice cream, to serve (optional)

SERVES 4

1 Preheat the oven to 350°F. Cut the peaches in half and remove the pits. With a spoon, scrape out some of the flesh from each peach half, slightly enlarging the hollow left by the pit. Chop this flesh and set it aside.

2 Put the amaretti cookies in a bowl and crush them finely with the end of a rolling pin.

3 Cream the low-fat spread and sugar together in a separate bowl until smooth. Stir in the reserved chopped peach flesh, the egg yolk and half the liqueur with the amaretti crumbs. Lightly grease a baking dish that is just large enough to hold the peach halves in a single layer.

NUTRITIONAL NOTES

Per portion:

Calories	232
Fat, total	5g
Saturated fat	1.37g
Cholesterol	54.7mg
Fiber	1.9g

4 Stand the peaches in the dish and spoon the stuffing into them. Mix the remaining liqueur with the wine, pour over the peaches and bake for 25 minutes or until the peaches feel tender. Decorate with basil and serve at once, with low-fat ice cream, if you like.

COCONUT DUMPLINGS WITH APRICOT SAUCE

—

These delicate little dumplings are very simple to make and cook in minutes. The sharp flavor of
the sauce offsets the creamy dumplings beautifully.

INGREDIENTS
6 tablespoons low-fat cottage cheese
1 egg white
1 tablespoon low-fat spread
1 tablespoon light brown sugar
2 tablespoons self-rising whole-wheat flour
finely grated zest of 1/2 lemon
1 tablespoon dried coconut, toasted

FOR THE SAUCE
*1 can (8 ounces) apricot halves in
natural juice*
1 tablespoon lemon juice

SERVES 4

1 Half-fill a steamer with boiling water
and put it on to boil. If you do not own
a steamer, place a heatproof plate over a
pan of boiling water.

NUTRITIONAL NOTES
Per portion:

Calories	112
Fat, total	4.3g
Saturated fat	2.56g
Cholesterol	1.2mg
Fiber	1.7g

2 Beat together the cottage cheese, egg
white and low-fat spread until they are
evenly mixed.

3 Stir in the sugar, flour, lemon zest and
coconut, mixing everything evenly to a
fairly firm dough.

4 Place 8–12 spoonfuls of the mixture in
the steamer or on the plate, leaving space
between them.

5 Cover the steamer or pan tightly with
a lid or a plate and steam for about
10 minutes, until the dumplings have
risen and are firm to the touch.

6 Meanwhile make the sauce. Purée the
can of apricots and stir in the lemon
juice. Pour into a small pan and heat until
boiling, then serve with the dumplings.
Sprinkle with extra coconut to serve, if
you like.

COOK'S TIP
The mixture should be quite stiff; if it
is not stiff enough to hold its shape, stir
in a little more flour.

PINEAPPLE FLAMBÉ

Flambéing means adding alcohol and then burning it off so the flavor is not too overpowering.
This dessert is just as good, however, without the brandy or vodka.

INGREDIENTS

1 ripe pineapple, about 1 pound 6 ounces
2 tablespoons low-fat spread
¼ cup light brown sugar
¼ cup fresh orange juice
2 tablespoons brandy or vodka
1 tablespoon slivered almonds, toasted

SERVES 4

1 Cut away the top and bottom of the pineapple. Then cut down the sides, removing all the dark "eyes."

2 Cut the pineapple into thin slices. Using an apple corer, remove the hard, central core from each slice.

VARIATION

Try this with nectarines, peaches or cherries. Omit the almonds if you want to reduce the fat content a little.

3 Melt the spread in a frying pan, with the sugar. Add the orange juice. Stir until hot, then add as many pineapple slices as the pan will hold and cook for 1–2 minutes, turning once. As each pineapple slice browns, remove it to a plate.

4 Return all the pineapple slices to the pan, heat briefly, then pour over the brandy or vodka and light with a long-handled match. Let the flames die down, then sprinkle with the almonds. Serve immediately.

NUTRITIONAL NOTES

Per portion:

Calories	171
Fat, total	5g
Saturated fat	0.62g
Cholesterol	0.4mg
Fiber	2.1g

WARM PEARS IN CIDER

—

There's no fat at all in this delectable dessert. Serve the pears with low-fat plain yogurt or fromage frais if you must, but they are very good on their own.

INGREDIENTS
1 lemon
¼ cup sugar
a little grated nutmeg
1 cup sweet cider
4 firm, ripe pears

SERVES 4

NUTRITIONAL NOTES
Per portion:

Calories	11
Fat, total	0g
Saturated fat	0g
Cholesterol	0mg
Fiber	3.3g

1 Using a potato peeler remove the zest from the lemon in thin strips, leaving any white pith behind.

2 Squeeze the juice from the lemon and pour it into a saucepan. Add the lemon zest, sugar, grated nutmeg and cider and heat gently until the sugar has completely dissolved.

3 Peel the pears, leaving the stems on if possible, and add them to the pan of cider. Poach the pears for 10–15 minutes, until almost tender, turning them frequently.

4 Transfer the pears to individual serving dishes using a slotted spoon. Simmer the liquid over a high heat until it reduces slightly and becomes syrupy. Pour the warm syrup over the pears. Serve immediately.

COOK'S TIP
To get pears of just the right firmness, you may have to buy them slightly underripe and then wait a day or more. Soft pears are no good at all for this dish.

FANNED POACHED PEARS IN PORT SYRUP

The perfect choice for autumn entertaining, this simple dessert has a beautiful rich color and
fantastic flavor thanks to the port and lemon.

INGREDIENTS

2 ripe, firm pears
pared zest of 1 lemon
3/4 cup ruby port
1/4 cup sugar
1 cinnamon stick
1/4 cup cold water
reduced-fat crème fraîche, to serve
(optional)

TO DECORATE

1 tablespoon sliced hazelnuts, toasted
fresh mint, pear or rose leaves

SERVES 4

1 Peel the pears, cut them in half and
remove the cores. Place the lemon zest,
port, sugar, cinnamon stick and water in a
shallow pan. Bring to a boil over low
heat. Add the pears, lower the heat, cover
and poach for 5 minutes. Let the pears
cool in the syrup.

NUTRITIONAL NOTES

Per portion:

Calories	173
Fat	2.5g
Saturated fat	0.17g
Cholesterol	0mg
Fiber	1.9g

2 When the pears are cold, transfer them
to a bowl with a slotted spoon. Return the
syrup to the heat. Boil rapidly until it has
reduced to form a syrup. Remove the
cinnamon stick and lemon zest and let the
syrup cool.

3 To serve, place each pear half in turn
on a board, cut side down. Keeping it
intact at the stem end, slice it lengthwise,
then, using a spatula, carefully lift it off
and place on a dessert plate. Press gently
so that the pear fans out. Spoon over the
port syrup. Top each portion with a few
hazelnuts and decorate with fresh mint,
pear or rose leaves. Serve immediately,
with reduced-fat crème fraîche, if you like.

MULLED PEARS WITH GINGER AND BRANDY

Serve these pears hot or cold, with lightly whipped cream. The flavors improve with keeping, so you can mull the pears several days before you want to serve them.

INGREDIENTS

2 1/2 cups red wine
1 cup sugar
1 cinnamon stick
6 cloves
finely grated zest of 1 orange
2 teaspoons grated fresh ginger
8 even-sized firm pears, with stems
1 tablespoon brandy
1/4 cup almonds or hazelnuts, toasted,
to decorate
low-fat whipped cream, to serve (optional)

SERVES 8

3 Gently remove the pears from the syrup with a slotted spoon, being very careful not to dislodge the stems. Put the cooked pears in a serving bowl or individual bowls, if you prefer.

NUTRITIONAL NOTES

Per portion:

Calories	246
Fat, total	1.9g
Saturated fat	0.13g
Cholesterol	0mg
Fiber	3.5g

4 Boil the syrup until it thickens and reduces. Cool slightly, add the brandy and strain over the pears. Decorate with toasted nuts. Serve with whipped cream, if you like.

1 Put all the ingredients except the pears, brandy and nuts into a large pan and heat slowly until the sugar has dissolved. Simmer for 5 minutes.

2 Peel the pears, leaving the stems on. Arrange them upright in the pan. Cover and simmer until tender, approximately 45–50 minutes, depending on size.

POACHED PEARS IN MAPLE-YOGURT SAUCE

An elegant dessert that is easier to make than it looks—poach the pears in advance, and have
the cooled syrup ready to spoon onto the plates just before you serve.

INGREDIENTS

6 firm dessert pears
1 tablespoon lemon juice
1 cup sweet white wine
or cider
thinly pared zest of 1 lemon
1 cinnamon stick
2 tablespoons maple syrup
1/2 teaspoon arrowroot
2/3 cup low-fat
plain yogurt

SERVES 6

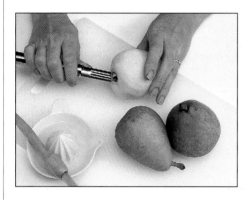

1 Peel the pears thinly, leaving them
whole and with the stems. Brush them
with lemon juice, to prevent them from
browning. Use a potato peeler or small
knife to scoop out the core from the
bottom of each pear.

2 Place the pears in a wide, heavy pan and
pour the wine or cider over, with enough
cold water to almost cover the pears.

3 Add the lemon zest and cinnamon
stick, then bring to a boil. Reduce the
heat, cover and simmer for 30–40 minutes,
or until tender. Turn the pears occasionally
so that they cook evenly. Lift out the pears
carefully, draining them well.

4 Boil the liquid uncovered to reduce to
about 1/2 cup. Strain into a bowl and add
the maple syrup. Blend a little of the
liquid with the arrowroot, then return the
mixture to the bowl; mix well. Return to
the pan and cook, stirring, until thick and
clear. Cool.

COOK'S TIP
The cooking time will vary, depending
upon the type and ripeness of the
pears. The pears should be ripe, but
still firm—over-ripe ones will not hold
their shape well.

5 Slice each pear about three-quarters
of the way through, leaving the slices
attached at the stem end. Fan each pear
out on a serving plate.

6 Stir 2 tablespoons of the cooled syrup
into the yogurt and spoon it around the
pears. Drizzle with the remaining syrup
and serve immediately.

NUTRITIONAL NOTES
Per portion:

Calories	136
Fat, total	1.4g
Saturated fat	0.79g
Cholesterol	1.8mg
Fiber	3.3g

BLUSHING PEARS

—

Pears poached in rosé wine and sweet spices absorb
all the subtle flavors and turn a soft pink color.

INGREDIENTS

6 firm pears
1¼ cups rosé wine
2/3 cup cranberry juice or apple juice
strip of thinly pared orange zest
1 cinnamon stick
4 whole cloves
1 bay leaf
5 tablespoons sugar
small bay leaves, to decorate

SERVES 6

1 Thinly peel the pears with a sharp
knife or vegetable peeler, leaving the
stems attached.

2 Pour the wine and cranberry or apple
juice into a large heavy saucepan. Add
the orange zest, cinnamon stick, cloves,
bay leaf and sugar.

3 Heat gently, stirring all the time until
the sugar has dissolved. Add the pears
and stand them upright in the pan. Pour
in enough cold water to barely cover
them. Cover and cook very gently for
20–30 minutes, or until just tender,
turning and basting occasionally.

4 Using a slotted spoon, gently lift the
pears out of the syrup and transfer to a
serving dish.

5 Bring the syrup to a boil and boil
rapidly for 10-15 minutes, or until it has
reduced by half.

6 Strain the syrup and pour over the
pears. Serve hot, decorated with
bay leaves.

NUTRITIONAL NOTES
Per portion:

Calories	148
Fat, total	0.16g
Saturated fat	0g
Cholesterol	0mg
Fiber	1.9g

COOK'S TIP

Check the pears by piercing with a
skewer or sharp knife towards the end
of the poaching time, because some
may cook more quickly than others.

CHAR-GRILLED APPLES ON CINNAMON TOASTS
—

**This yummy treat makes a fabulous finale to a summer barbecue,
but it can also be cooked under the grill.**

INGREDIENTS

4 sweet apples
juice of 1/2 lemon
4 individual English muffins
1 tablespoon low-fat spread, melted
2 tablespoons light brown sugar
1 teaspoon ground cinnamon
low-fat plain yogurt, to serve (optional)

SERVES 4

1 Core the apples and cut them horizontally in three or four thick slices. Sprinkle with lemon juice.

VARIATION
Other fruit in season could be used for this recipe. Try pears, peaches or pineapple for variety. Nutmeg or apple pie spice could also replace the cinnamon.

NUTRITIONAL NOTES
Per portion:

Calories	241
Fat, total	4.9g
Saturated fat	1.63g
Cholesterol	0.2mg
Fiber	3.0g

2 Cut the English muffins into thick slices. Brush sparingly with melted low-fat spread on both sides.

3 Mix together the sugar and ground cinnamon. Preheat the broiler if not using an outdoor grill.

4 Place the apple and muffin slices on the hot grill or under the broiler and cook them for 3–4 minutes, turning once, until they are beginning to turn golden brown.

5 Sprinkle half the cinnamon sugar over the apple slices and toasts and cook for 1 minute more, until they are a rich golden brown.

6 To serve, arrange the apple slices over the toasts and sprinkle them with the remaining cinnamon sugar. Serve hot, with low-fat plain yogurt, if you like.

COOK'S TIP
To keep the quantity of fat within acceptable levels, make this simple, scrumptious dessert with muffins, but for a splurge, use brioche or a similar sweet bread.

COOL FRUIT DESSERTS

On a warm summer's day what could be more refreshing than a luscious fruit dessert making the most of fresh seasonal produce, and yet still remaining deliciously low in fat?

RICH BLACK CURRANT COULIS

There can be few more impressive desserts than this—
port wine jelly with swirled cream hearts.

INGREDIENTS
3 packages powdered gelatin
2 cups water
1 pound black currants
1 cup sugar
2/3 cup ruby port
2 tablespoons crème de cassis
1/2 cup light cream,
to decorate

SERVES 8

1 In a small bowl, soak the gelatin in 5 tablespoons of the water until soft. Place the black currants, sugar and 1¼ cups of the remaining water in a large saucepan. Bring to a boil, lower the heat and simmer for 20 minutes.

2 Strain, reserving the cooking liquid in a large bowl. Put half the black currants in a bowl and pour over ¼ cup of the reserved cooking liquid. (Freeze the remaining black currants for another day.) Set the two bowls aside.

3 Pour softened gelatin in a small saucepan with the port, cassis and remaining water. Heat gently to dissolve the gelatin but do not allow the mixture to boil. Stir the gelatin mixture into the bowl of black currant liquid until well mixed.

4 Run 6–8 jelly molds under cold water, drain and place in a roasting pan. Fill with the port mixture. Chill for at least 6 hours, until set. Pour the bowl of black currants into a food processor, purée until smooth, then pass through a fine sieve. Taste the coulis and adjust the sweetness.

5 Run a fine knife around each jelly. Dip each mold in hot water for 5–10 seconds, then turn the jelly out onto a serving plate and spoon the coulis around the jelly.

6 To decorate, drop a little cream at intervals onto the coulis. Draw a toothpick through the cream dots, dragging each in turn into a heart shape. Serve the desserts immediately.

NUTRITIONAL NOTES
Per portion:

Calories	276
Fat, total	3.8g
Saturated fat	2.4g
Cholesterol	11mg
Fiber	2.7g

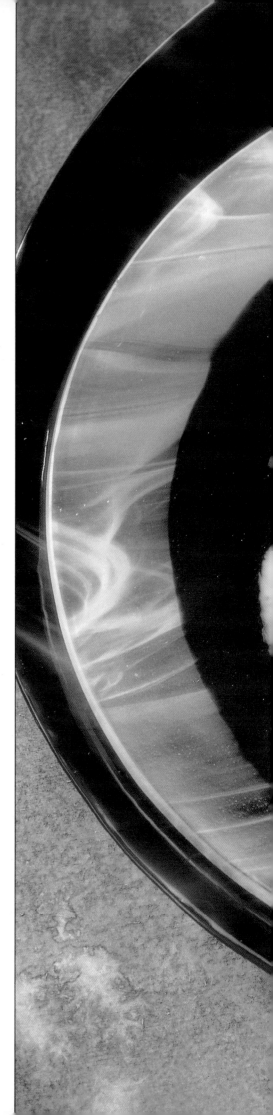

STRAWBERRIES IN SPICED GRAPE JELLY

The spicy cinnamon combines with the sun-ripened strawberries to make a delectable dessert for a summer dinner party.

INGREDIENTS
2 cups red grape juice
1 cinnamon stick
1 small orange
1 tablespoon powdered gelatin
2 cups strawberries, chopped, plus extra to decorate

SERVES 4

1 Pour the grape juice into a pan and add the cinnamon stick. Thinly pare the zest from the orange. Add most of it to the pan but shred some pieces and set them aside for the decoration. Place the pan over very low heat for 10 minutes, then remove the flavorings from the grape juice.

2 Squeeze the juice from the orange into a bowl and sprinkle over the powdered gelatin. When the mixture is spongy, stir into the grape juice until it has completely dissolved. Allow the jelly to cool in the bowl until just beginning to set.

3 Stir in the strawberries and quickly pour into a 4-cup mold or serving dish. Chill until set.

4 Dip the mold quickly into hot water and invert on to a serving plate. Decorate with strawberries and shreds of orange rind.

NUTRITIONAL NOTES
Per portion:

Calories	85
Fat, total	0.2g
Saturated fat	0g
Cholesterol	0mg
Fiber	1.04g

CHILLED ORANGES IN SYRUP

This popular classic is light and simple to make, refreshing and delicious.
A perfect dish to serve after a heavy main course.

2 Cut the orange zest into fine strips and boil in water several times to remove the bitterness. Drain on paper towels.

3 Place the water, sugar and lemon juice in a saucepan. Bring to a boil, add the pared orange zest and simmer until the syrup thickens. Add the orange-flower or rose-water, stir and let cool.

INGREDIENTS

4 oranges
2¹/2 cups water
1¹/2 cups granulated sugar
2 tablespoons lemon juice
2 tablespoons orange-flower water or rose-water
¹/3 cup unsalted pistachios, shelled and chopped

SERVES 4

1 Peel the oranges with a potato peeler, avoiding the pith.

NUTRITIONAL NOTES

Per portion:

Calories	467
Fat, total	4.9g
Saturated fat	0.59g
Cholesterol	0mg
Fiber	3.1g

COOK'S TIP

Almonds could be substituted for the pistachios, if you like, but don't be tempted to increase the quantity or you'll raise the amount of fat.

4 Peel away the orange pith and slice. Arrange in a serving dish and pour the syrup over. Chill for 1–2 hours. Sprinkle the pistachios over before serving.

GRAPES IN GRAPE-YOGURT JELLY

—

This light, refreshing combination makes a great special-occasion dessert,
but takes very little time to make.

INGREDIENTS

1¾ cups seedless green grapes
scant 2 cups unsweetened
white grape juice
1 tablespoon powdered gelatin
½ cup low-fat plain yogurt

SERVES 4

1 Set aside four tiny bunches of grapes
for decoration. Pull the rest off their
stems and cut them in half.

2 Divide the grapes among four stem
glasses and tilt the glasses on one side,
propping them firmly in a bowl of ice.

3 Place the grape juice in a pan and heat
it until almost boiling. Remove it from the
heat and sprinkle the gelatin over the
surface, stirring to dissolve the gelatin.

4 Pour half the grape juice over the
grapes and let set.

5 Cool the remaining grape juice until
on the verge of setting, then stir in the
low-fat plain yogurt.

6 Stand the set glasses upright and pour
in the yogurt mixture. Chill to set, then
decorate the rim of each glass with
grapes, and serve.

NUTRITIONAL NOTES
Per portion:

Calories	113
Fat, total	0.4g
Saturated fat	0.16g
Cholesterol	1.3mg
Fiber	0g

COOK'S TIP
For an easier version, stand the glasses
upright rather than at an angle—then
they can be put in the refrigerator to
set rather than packed with ice.

FRESH CITRUS JELLY

Fresh fruit jellies really are worth the effort—they're packed with fresh flavor, natural color and vitamins—and they make a lovely fat-free dessert.

INGREDIENTS
3 medium oranges
1 lemon
1 lime
1¼ cups water
6 tablespoons demerara sugar
1 tablespoon powdered gelatin
extra slices of citrus fruit,
to decorate

SERVES 4

1 With a sharp knife, cut all the zest and white pith from one orange and carefully remove the segments. Arrange the segments in the bottom of a 3¾-cup mold or dish. Chill.

2 Remove some shreds of citrus zest with a zester and reserve them for decoration. Grate the remaining zest from the lemon and lime and one orange. Place all the grated zest in a medium-sized pan, with the water and sugar.

3 Heat gently, without boiling, until the sugar has dissolved. Remove from heat. Squeeze the juice from all the rest of the fruit and stir it into the pan.

4 Strain the hot liquid into a measuring cup to remove the zest. You should have about 2½ cups of liquid; if necessary, make up the amount with hot water. Sprinkle the gelatin over the liquid and stir until it has dissolved completely.

5 Pour a little of the jelly over the orange segments and chill until set. Leave the remaining jelly at room temperature to cool, but do not allow it to set.

6 Pour the remaining cooled jelly into the dish and chill until set. To serve, turn out the jelly and decorate it with the reserved citrus zest shreds and extra slices of citrus fruit.

COOK'S TIP
To speed up the setting of the fruit segments in jelly, stand the dish in a bowl of ice. Or, if you're short of time, simply stir the segments into the liquid jelly, pour into a serving dish and set it all together.

NUTRITIONAL NOTES
Per portion:

Calories	137
Fat, total	0.2g
Saturated fat	0g
Cholesterol	0mg
Fiber	2.1g

ORANGE-BLOSSOM JELLY

A fresh orange jelly makes a delightful dessert; the natural fruit flavor combined with the smooth jelly has a wonderful cleansing quality.

INGREDIENTS
5 tablespoons sugar
2/3 cup water
1 ounce powdered gelatin
2 1/2 cups fresh orange juice
2 tablespoons orange-flower water

SERVES 4

3 Gently melt the gelatin over a saucepan of simmering water until it becomes clear and transparent. Let cool. When the gelatin is cold, mix it with the orange juice and orange-flower water.

1 Place the sugar and water in a small saucepan and heat gently to dissolve the sugar. Pour into a heatproof bowl and let cool.

4 Wet a jelly mold and pour in the jelly. Chill in the refrigerator for at least 2 hours, or until set. Turn out to serve. If the jelly is difficult to remove, place the mold in warm water for a few seconds and the jelly should come out easily.

2 Sprinkle the gelatin over the surface of the syrup. Let stand until the gelatin has absorbed all the liquid.

COOK'S TIP
If you are entertaining, make this jelly extra-special by substituting Grand Marnier for the orange-flower water.

NUTRITIONAL NOTES
Per portion:

Calories	135
Fat, total	0g
Saturated fat	0g
Cholesterol	0mg
Fiber	0.2g

CLEMENTINE JELLY

—

Jelly isn't only for children; this adult version has a clear fruity taste and can be made extra
special by adding a little white rum or Cointreau.

2 Pour half the juice mixture into a pan.
Sprinkle the gelatin on top, set aside for
5 minutes, then heat gently until the
gelatin has dissolved. Stir in the sugar,
then the remaining juice; set aside.

3 Pare the zest very thinly from the
remaining fruit and set it aside. Using a
sharp knife, cut between the membrane
and fruit to separate the citrus segments.
Discard the membrane and pith.

4 Place half the segments in four dessert
glasses and cover with some of the liquid
fruit jelly. Place in the refrigerator to set.

INGREDIENTS
12 clementines
clear unsweetened white grape juice
(see method for amount)
1 tablespoon powdered gelatin
2 tablespoons sugar
¼ cup reduced-fat crème fraîche,
for topping

SERVES 4

1 Squeeze the juice from eight of the
clementines and pour it into a bowl.
Make up to 2½ cups with the grape
juice, then strain the juice mixture
through a fine sieve.

5 Arrange the remaining segments on
top. Carefully pour over the remaining
liquid jelly and chill until set. Cut the
pared clementine zest into shreds. Serve
the jellies topped with a spoonful of
crème fraîche scattered with clementine
zest shreds.

NUTRITIONAL NOTES
Per portion:

Calories	142
Fat, total	2.5g
Saturated fat	1.4g
Cholesterol	15.8mg
Fiber	1.5g

VARIATION
Use ruby grapefruit instead of
clementines, if you prefer. Squeeze the
juice from half and segment the rest.

MEXICAN LEMONY RICE PUDDING

Rice pudding is popular the world over and is always different. This Mexican version is light and
very easy to make.

INGREDIENTS

¹/2 cup raisins

*¹/2 cup short-grain
(pudding) rice*

*1-inch strip of pared lime or
lemon zest*

1 cup water

2 cups skim milk

1 cup sugar

¹/4 teaspoon salt

1-inch cinnamon stick

1 egg yolk, well beaten

1 tablespoon low-fat spread

*2 teaspoons toasted flaked almonds
to decorate*

orange segments to serve

SERVES 4

3 Discard the cinnamon stick. Drain the
raisins well. Add the raisins, egg yolk and
low-fat spread, stirring constantly until
the spread has been absorbed and the
pudding is rich and creamy.

4 Cook the pudding for a few minutes
longer. Place the rice in a serving dish
and allow to cool. Decorate with the
toasted flaked almonds and serve with
the orange segments.

NUTRITIONAL NOTES
Per portion:

Calories	450
Fat, total	4.9g
Saturated fat	0.88g
Cholesterol	53mg
Fiber	1.4g

1 Put the raisins in a small bowl. Cover
with warm water and set aside to soak.
Put the rice into a saucepan together with
the pared lime or lemon zest and water.
Bring slowly to a boil, then lower the
heat. Cover the pan and simmer gently for
about 20 minutes or until all the water
has been absorbed.

2 Remove the zest from the rice and
discard it. Add the milk, sugar, salt and
cinnamon stick. Cook, stirring, over very
low heat until all the milk has been
absorbed. Do not cover the pan.

FRAGRANT RICE PUDDING WITH DATES

The rice puddings that are popular all over Morocco are served liberally sprinkled with either
nuts and honey or wrapped in pastry. This is a low-fat version.

INGREDIENTS

1/2 cup short-grain (pudding) rice

about 3³/4 cups

skim milk

2 tablespoons ground rice

1/4 cup sugar

2 tablespoons ground almonds

1 teaspoon vanilla extract

1/2 teaspoon pure almond extract

a little orange-flower water (optional)

2 tablespoons chopped dates

2 tablespoons unsalted, pistachios,

finely chopped

SERVES 4

1 Place the rice in a saucepan with
3 cups of the milk and gradually heat
until simmering. Cook, uncovered,
over very low heat for 30–40 minutes,
until the rice is completely tender,
stirring frequently.

NUTRITIONAL NOTES
Per portion:

Calories	270
Fat, total	4.8g
Saturated fat	0.55g
Cholesterol	4.5mg
Fiber	0.4g

2 Blend the ground rice with the
remaining milk and add to the pan,
stirring. Slowly bring back to a boil
and cook for 1 minute.

3 Stir in the sugar, ground almonds,
vanilla and almond extracts and orange-
flower water, if using. Cook until the
pudding is thick and creamy.

4 Pour into serving bowls and sprinkle
with the chopped dates and pistachios.
Allow to cool before serving.

RICE PUDDING WITH MIXED BERRY SAUCE

—

**A compote of red berries contrasts beautifully with creamy rice pudding
for a richly flavored cool dessert.**

INGREDIENTS

low-fat spread, for greasing
2 cups short-grain
(pudding) rice
scant 1 1/2 cups
skim milk
pinch salt
2/3 cup light brown sugar
1 teaspoon pure vanilla extract
2 eggs, beaten
grated zest of 1 lemon
1 teaspoon lemon juice
2 tablespoons low-fat spread
strawberry leaves, to decorate

FOR THE SAUCE

2 cups strawberries, hulled
and quartered
2 cups raspberries
1/2 cup granulated sugar
grated zest of 1 lemon

SERVES 6

1 Preheat the oven to 325°F. Grease a deep 8-cup baking dish. Add the rice to boiling water and boil for 5 minutes. Drain. Transfer the rice to the prepared baking dish.

2 Combine the milk, salt, brown sugar, vanilla extract, eggs, and lemon zest and juice. Pour over the rice and stir.

3 Dot the surface of the rice mixture with the spread. Bake for about 50 minutes until the rice is cooked and creamy.

4 Meanwhile, make the sauce. Mix the berries and sugar in a small saucepan. Stir over low heat until the sugar dissolves completely and the fruit is becoming pulpy.

5 Transfer to a bowl and stir in the lemon zest. Cool, then chill until required.

6 Remove the rice pudding from the oven. Let cool. Serve with the berry sauce. Decorate with strawberry leaves.

NUTRITIONAL NOTES
Per portion:

Calories	474
Fat, total	4.9g
Saturated fat	0.95g
Cholesterol	65.5mg
Fiber	1.4g

FRESH FRUIT WITH CARAMEL RICE

Creamy rice pudding with a crisp caramel crust sounds wickedly indulgent, but is relatively low in fat, especially if you serve fairly small portions, with fresh fruit.

INGREDIENTS
¹/4 cup short-grain (pudding) rice
low-fat spread, for greasing
5 tablespoons demerara sugar
pinch of salt
1 can (14 ounces) light evaporated milk
made up to 2¹/2 cups with water
2 crisp apples
1 small fresh pineapple
2 teaspoon lemon juice

SERVES 4

3 Meanwhile, peel, core and cut the apples and pineapple into thin slices, then cut the pineapple into chunks. Toss the fruit in lemon juice, coating thoroughly, and set aside.

4 Preheat the broiler and sprinkle the remaining sugar over the rice. Broil for 5 minutes to caramelize the sugar. Let stand for 5 minutes to harden the caramel. Serve with the fresh fruit.

1 Preheat the oven to 300°F. Wash the rice under cold water. Drain well and put into a lightly greased soufflé dish.

2 Add 2 tablespoons of the sugar to the dish, with the salt. Pour in the diluted evaporated milk and stir gently. Bake for 2 hours, then let cool for 30 minutes.

NUTRITIONAL NOTES
Per portion:

Calories	309
Fat, total	4.6g
Saturated fat	2.51g
Cholesterol	34mg
Fiber	2.8g

RICE FRUIT SUNDAE

—

Cook a rice pudding on top of the stove instead of in the oven for a light creamy texture.
It is particularly good served cold topped with fruits.

INGREDIENTS
1/3 cup short-grain
(pudding) rice
2 1/2 cups skim milk
1 teaspoon pure vanilla extract
1/2 teaspoon ground cinnamon
2 tablespoons granulated sugar
1 3/4 cups strawberries, raspberries or
blueberries, to serve

SERVES 4

1 Put the rice, milk, vanilla extract, cinnamon and sugar into a medium-sized saucepan. Bring to a boil, stirring constantly, and then turn down the heat so that the mixture barely simmers.

2 Cook the rice for 30–40 minutes, stirring occasionally, until the grains are soft. Pour into a bowl and allow the rice to cool, stirring occasionally. When cold, chill the rice in the refrigerator.

NUTRITIONAL NOTES
Per portion:

Calories	169
Fat, total	3.3g
Saturated fat	0.1g
Cholesterol	3mg
Fiber	0.9g

3 Just before serving, stir the rice and spoon into four sundae dishes. Top with the prepared fruit.

VARIATION
Instead of simple pudding rice try using a Thai fragrant or jasmine rice for a delicious natural flavor. For a firmer texture, an Italian arborio rice makes a good pudding too. You could also use other toppings, such as toasted, chopped hazelnuts or toasted coconut flakes. Other fruit combinations could be mango, pineapple and banana for a tropical taste.

SUMMER PUDDING

—

**Summer pudding is an annual treat, and need not be high in fat if you avoid serving it
with heavy cream.**

2 Pour the red currant mixture into a food
processor and process until quite smooth.
Press through a fine-mesh nylon strainer
set in a bowl. Discard the fruit pulp left in
the strainer.

3 Put the mixed berries in a bowl with the
remaining sugar and the lemon juice.
Stir well.

4 One at a time, remove the cut bread
pieces from the bowl and dip them in the
red currant purée. Replace to line the
bowl evenly.

5 Spoon the berries into the lined bowl,
pressing them down evenly. Top with the
reserved cut bread slices, which have
been dipped in the red currant purée.

6 Cover the bowl with plastic wrap.
Set a small plate, just big enough to fit
inside the rim of the bowl, on top of the
pudding. Weigh it down with cans of food.
Chill in the refrigerator for 8–24 hours.

7 To turn out, remove the weights, plate
and plastic wrap. Run a knife between
the bowl and the pudding to loosen it.
Invert on to a serving plate. Decorate with
a sprig of mint and a few berries. Serve
in wedges.

INGREDIENTS

*1 loaf of white crusty bread,
1–2 days old, sliced
6 cups fresh red currants
6 tablespoons granulated sugar
1/4 cup water
4 cups mixed berries, plus extra to decorate
sprig of mint, to decorate
juice of 1/2 lemon*

SERVES 6

NUTRITIONAL NOTES

Per portion:

Calories	272
Fat, total	1.6g
Saturated fat	0g
Cholesterol	0mg
Fiber	7.6g

1 Trim the crusts from the bread slices.
Cut a round of bread to fit in the bottom of
a 6-cup pudding bowl. Line the bowl with
bread slices, overlapping them slightly.
Reserve enough bread slices to cover the
top of the bowl. Mix the red currants with
1/4 cup of the sugar and the water in a
nonreactive saucepan. Heat gently,
crushing the berries lightly to help the
juices flow. When the sugar has dissolved,
remove from heat.

AUTUMN PUDDING

Summer pudding is far too good to be reserved for the soft fruit season. Here is an autumn
version, with apples, plums and blackberries.

INGREDIENTS
1 pound apples
1 pound plums, halved and pitted
2 cups blackberries
¹/4 cup apple juice
sugar or honey, to sweeten (optional)
8 slices of whole-wheat bread, crusts removed
mint sprig and blackberry, to decorate
reduced-fat crème fraîche, to serve
(optional)
SERVES 6

3 Spoon the fruit into the bowl. Pour in
just enough juice to moisten. Reserve any
remaining juice.

4 Cover the fruit completely with the
remaining bread. Fit a plate on top, so
that it rests on the bread just below the
rim. Stand the bowl in a larger bowl to
catch any juice. Place a weight on the
plate and chill overnight.

5 Turn the pudding out onto a plate and
pour the reserved juice over any areas
that have not absorbed the juice.
Decorate with the mint sprig and
blackberry. Serve with crème fraîche,
if you like.

1 Quarter the apples, remove the cores
and peel, then slice them into a saucepan.
Add the plums, blackberries and apple
juice. Cover and cook gently for
10–15 minutes, until tender. Sweeten, if
necessary, with a little sugar or honey,
although the fruit should be sweet enough.

2 Line the bottom and sides of a
5-cup pudding bowl with slices of bread,
cut to fit. Press together tightly.

NUTRITIONAL NOTES
Per portion:

Calories	141
Fat, total	1.1g
Saturated fat	0.17g
Cholesterol	0mg
Fiber	5.4g

TWO-TONE YOGURT RING WITH TROPICAL FRUIT

An impressive, light and colorful dessert with a truly tropical flavor,
combining mango, kiwi fruit and Cape gooseberries together.

INGREDIENTS

3/4 cup tropical fruit juice
1 tablespoon powdered gelatin
3 egg whites
2/3 cup low-fat
plain yogurt
finely grated zest of 1 lime

FOR THE FILLING

1 mango
2 kiwi fruit
10–12 Cape gooseberries,
plus extra to decorate
juice of 1 lime

SERVES 6

1 Pour the tropical fruit juice into a small pan and sprinkle the powdered gelatin over the surface. Heat gently until the gelatin has dissolved.

NUTRITIONAL NOTES

Per portion:

Calories	87
Fat, total	0.5g
Saturated fat	0.13g
Cholesterol	1mg
Fiber	2.3g

2 Beat the egg whites in a grease-free bowl until they hold soft peaks. Continue beating hard, gradually adding the yogurt and lime zest.

3 Continue beating hard and pour in the hot gelatin mixture in a steady stream, until evenly mixed.

4 Quickly pour the mixture into a 6¼-cup ring mold. Chill the mold in the refrigerator until set. The mixture will separate into two layers.

5 Prepare the filling. Halve, pit, peel and dice the mango. Peel and slice the kiwi fruit. Remove the husks from the Cape gooseberries and cut them in half. Toss all the fruits together in a bowl and stir in the lime juice.

6 Run a knife around the edge of the ring to loosen the mixture. Dip the ring mold quickly into hot water, then turn it out on to a serving plate. Spoon all the prepared fruit into the center of the ring, decorate with the reserved Cape gooseberries and serve immediately.

VARIATION

Any mixture of fruit works in
this recipe, depending on the season.
Try using apple juice in the ring
mixture and fill it with luscious,
red summer fruits.

FRUITED RICE RING

This unusual rice pudding looks beautiful turned out of a ring mold but if you prefer, stir the fruit into the rice and serve in individual dishes.

2 Meanwhile, mix the dried fruit salad and orange juice in a pan and bring to a boil. Cover, then simmer very gently for about 1 hour, until tender and no free liquid remains.

3 Remove the cinnamon stick from the rice and stir in the sugar and orange zest, mixing thoroughly.

4 Pour the fruit into the bottom of a lightly oiled 6¼-cup ring mold. Spoon the rice over, smoothing down firmly. Chill.

5 Run a knife around the edge of the mold and turn out the rice carefully onto a serving plate.

INGREDIENTS

*5 tablespoons short-grain
(pudding) rice
3¾ cups low-fat milk
1 cinnamon stick
1½ cups dried fruit salad
1½ cups orange juice
3 tablespoons sugar
finely grated zest of 1 small orange
oil, for greasing*

SERVES 4

1 Mix the rice, milk and cinnamon stick in a large pan and bring to a boil. Lower the heat, cover and simmer, stirring occasionally, for about 1½ hours, until no free liquid remains.

NUTRITIONAL NOTES
Per portion:

Calories	343
Fat, total	4.4g
Saturated fat	2.26g
Cholesterol	15.75mg
Fiber	1.07g

DRIED FRUIT FOOL

—

This light, fluffy dessert can be made with a single dried fruit—try dried peaches,
prunes, apples or apricots.

INGREDIENTS

1¼ cups
dried fruit
such as apricots, peaches, prunes or apples
1¼ cups fresh orange juice
1 cup low-fat fromage frais
2 egg whites
fresh mint sprigs, to decorate

SERVES 4

NUTRITIONAL NOTES

Per portion:

Calories	180
Fat, total	0.63g
Saturated fat	0.06g
Cholesterol	0.5mg
Fiber	4.8g

3 Beat the egg whites in a greasefree bowl until stiff enough to hold soft peaks, then slowly fold into the fruit mixture until it is all combined.

4 Spoon into four stem glasses or one large serving dish. Chill for at least 1 hour. Decorate with the mint sprigs just before serving.

COOK'S TIP
To make a speedier fool leave out the egg whites and simply swirl together the fruit mixture and fromage frais.

1 Put the dried fruit in a saucepan, add the orange juice and heat gently until boiling. Lower the heat, cover and simmer gently for 3 minutes.

2 Cool slightly. Pour into a food processor or blender and process until smooth. Stir in the fromage frais.

PASSION FRUIT AND APPLE FOAM

Passion fruit have an exotic, scented flavor that really lifts this simple apple dessert.
If passion fruit are not available, use two finely chopped kiwis instead.

INGREDIENTS
1 pound cooking apples
6 tablespoons unsweetened apple juice
3 passion fruits
3 egg whites
1 red-skinned apple, to decorate
1 teaspoon lemon juice

SERVES 4

1 Peel, core and roughly chop the cooking apples. Put them in a pan with the apple juice.

2 Bring the liquid to a boil, then lower the heat and cover the pan. Cook gently, stirring occasionally, until the apple is very tender.

3 Remove from heat and beat the apple mixture with a wooden spoon until it forms a fairly smooth purée (or purée the apple in a food processor if you prefer).

4 Cut the passion fruit in half and scoop out the flesh. Stir the flesh into the apple purée to mix thoroughly.

5 Place the egg whites in a greasefree bowl and beat them until they form soft peaks. Fold the egg whites into the apple mixture. Spoon the apple foam into four serving dishes. Let cool.

6 Thinly slice the red-skinned apple and brush the slices with lemon juice to prevent them from browning. Arrange the slices on top of the apple foam and serve cold.

COOK'S TIP
It is important to use a good cooking apple, such as an Ida Red, for this recipe, because the fluffy texture of a cooking apple breaks down easily to a purée. You can use dessert apples, but will probably have to purée them in a food processor.

NUTRITIONAL NOTES
Per portion:

Calories	80
Fat, total	0.2g
Saturated fat	0g
Cholesterol	0mg
Fiber	2.9g .

RASPBERRY AND MINT BAVAROIS

A sophisticated dessert that can be made a day in advance for a special
dinner party.

INGREDIENTS

*4 cups fresh or
thawed frozen raspberries
2 tablespoons confectioners' sugar
2 tablespoons lemon juice
1 tablespoon finely chopped fresh mint
2 tablespoons powdered gelatin
5 tablespoons boiling water
1¼ cups low-fat custard
1 cup low-fat plain yogurt
fresh mint sprigs, to decorate*

SERVES 6

2 Press the purée through a sieve to
remove the raspberry seeds. Pour it into
a measuring cup and stir in the mint.

5 Mix the custard and low-fat plain
yogurt in a bowl and stir in the remaining
fruit purée. Dissolve the rest of the
gelatin in the remaining boiling water and
stir it in quickly.

1 Reserve a few raspberries for
decoration. Place the remaining
raspberries in a food processor. Add the
confectioners' sugar and lemon juice and
process to a smooth purée.

3 Sprinkle 1 teaspoon of the gelatin over
2 tablespoons of the boiling water and stir
until the gelatin has dissolved. Stir into
⅔ cup of the fruit purée.

6 Pour the raspberry custard into the
mold and chill it until it has set
completely. To serve, dip the mold
quickly into hot water and then turn it out
on a serving plate. Decorate with the
reserved raspberries and the mint sprigs.

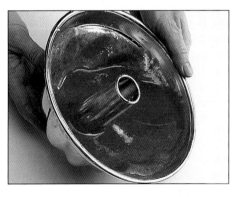

4 Pour this jelly into a 4-cup mold, and
chill in the refrigerator until the jelly is
just setting. Rotate the mold to swirl the
setting jelly around the sides, and let chill
until the jelly has set completely.

NUTRITIONAL NOTES
Per portion:

Calories	131
Fat, total	2.4g
Saturated fat	1.36g
Cholesterol	4.1mg
Fiber	1.9g

COOK'S TIP
You can make this dessert using frozen
raspberries, which have a good color
and flavor. Allow them to thaw at room
temperature, and use any juice
in the jelly.

BRAZILIAN COFFEE BANANAS

—

Rich, lavish and luscious, this low-fat dessert takes only about
2 minutes to make!

INGREDIENTS
4 small ripe bananas
1 tablespoon instant coffee granules
or powder
1 tablespoon hot water
2 tablespoons dark muscovado sugar
1 cup low-fat plain yogurt
2 teaspoons toasted flaked almonds

SERVES 4

NUTRITIONAL NOTES
Per portion:

Calories	175
Fat, total	4.8g
Saturated fat	2.06g
Cholesterol	4.4mg
Fiber	1.1g

1 Peel and slice one banana and peel and
mash the remaining three with a fork.
Dissolve the coffee in the hot water and
stir into the mashed bananas.

VARIATION
For a special occasion, add a dash of
dark rum or brandy to the bananas.
1 tablespoon of rum or brandy won't affect
the amount of fat, but will add 30 calories.

2 Spoon a little of the mashed banana
mixture into four serving dishes and
sprinkle each with sugar. Top with a
spoonful of yogurt, then repeat the layers
until all the ingredients are used up.

3 Swirl the last layer of yogurt for a
marbled effect. Finish with a few banana
slices and flaked almonds. Serve cold.
This dish is best eaten within about an
hour of making.

RASPBERRY MUESLI LAYER

As well as being a delicious, low-fat dessert, this can be made in advance
and stored in the refrigerator overnight to be served for a quick, healthy breakfast.

INGREDIENTS

*2 cups fresh or frozen and
thawed raspberries
1 cup low-fat plain yogurt
1/2 cup Swiss-style muesli*

SERVES 4

3 Sprinkle a layer of Swiss-style muesli
over the yogurt.

4 Continue the layers until all the
ingredients have been used. Top each
dessert with a whole raspberry.

1 Reserve four raspberries for decoration,
then spoon a few raspberries into four
stem glasses or glass dishes.

2 Top the raspberries in each glass with a
spoonful of yogurt.

NUTRITIONAL NOTES
Per portion:

Calories	114
Fat, total	1.7g
Saturated fat	0.48g
Cholesterol	2.3mg
Fiber	2.6g

CLEMENTINES IN CINNAMON CARAMEL

The combination of sweet, yet sharp clementines and caramel sauce with a hint of spice is divine.
Served with low-fat plain yogurt or crème fraîche, this makes a delicious dessert.

INGREDIENTS

8–12 clementines, about
1–1¼ pounds
1 cup sugar
1¼ cups warm water
2 cinnamon sticks
2 tablespoons orange-flavored liqueur
¼ cup shelled unsalted
pistachios

SERVES 4

1 Using a vegetable peeler, pare the zest from two clementines and cut it into fine strips. Set aside.

2 Peel the clementines, removing all the pith but keeping each fruit intact. Put the fruits in a heatproof serving bowl.

3 Gently heat the sugar in a pan until it dissolves and turns a rich golden brown. Immediately turn off the heat.

4 Protecting your hand with a dish towel, carefully pour in the warm water (the mixture will bubble and splutter). Bring slowly to a boil, stirring until all the caramel has dissolved.

5 Add the shredded peel and cinnamon sticks, then simmer for 5 minutes. Stir in the orange-flavored liqueur.

6 Let the syrup to cool for about 10 minutes, then pour it over the clementines. Cover the bowl, cool, then chill for several hours or overnight.

7 Blanch the unsalted pistachios in boiling water. Drain, cool and remove outer skins. Decorate the clementines by scattering the nuts over the top. Serve immediately.

NUTRITIONAL NOTES
Per portion:

Calories	328
Fat, total	3.5g
Saturated fat	0.42g
Cholesterol	0mg
Fiber	1.4g

YOGURT WITH APRICOTS AND PISTACHIOS
—

If you allow a yogurt to drain overnight, it becomes thicker and more luscious. Add honeyed apricots and nuts, and you have an exotic yet simple dessert.

INGREDIENTS
2 cups low-fat plain yogurt
3/4 cup dried apricots, snipped
1 tablespoon honey
2 teaspoons roughly chopped unsalted pistachios, plus extra for sprinkling
ground cinnamon, for sprinkling

SERVES 4

1 Place the yogurt in a sieve over a bowl. Drain overnight in the refrigerator.

2 Discard the yogurt whey. Place the apricots in a saucepan, cover with water and simmer to soften. Drain, cool, then pour into a bowl and stir in the honey.

3 Add the yogurt to the apricot mixture, with the nuts. Spoon into sundae dishes, sprinkle a little cinnamon and the nuts over and chill. Serve chilled.

NUTRITIONAL NOTES
Per portion:

Calories	164
Fat, total	4.5g
Saturated fat	2g
Cholesterol	5.5mg
Fiber	2.8g

RASPBERRIES AND FRUIT PURÉE

Three fruit purées, swirled together, make a
kaleidoscopic garnish for a nest of raspberries.

INGREDIENTS
7 ounces raspberries
1/2 cup red wine
confectioners' sugar, for dusting

FOR THE DECORATION
1 large mango, peeled and chopped
14 ounces kiwi fruit, peeled and chopped
7 ounces raspberries
confectioners' sugar, to taste

SERVES 4–6

1 Place the raspberries in a bowl with the
red wine and allow to macerate for about
2 hours.

2 Make the decoration. Purée the mango
in a food processor, adding water if
necessary. Press through a sieve into a
bowl. Purée the kiwi fruit in the same way,
then make a third purée from the remaining
raspberries. Sweeten the purées with
sifted confectioners' sugar, if necessary.

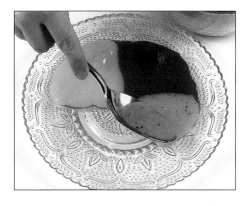

3 Spoon each purée on to a serving plate,
separating the kiwi and mango with the
raspberry purée as if creating a four-
wedged pie. Gently tap the plate on the
work surface to settle the purées against
each other.

4 Using a skewer, draw a spiral outwards
from the center of the plate to the rim.
Drain the macerated raspberries, pile
them in the center, and dust them heavily
with confectioners' sugar.

NUTRITIONAL NOTES
Per portion:

Calories	154
Fat, total	0.9g
Saturated fat	0g
Cholesterol	0mg
Fiber	6.7g

CRIMSON PEARS

—

Poached pears in red wine are among the simplest of sweet treats,
but they look spectacular.

INGREDIENTS

1 bottle of red wine
3/4 cup sugar
3 tablespoons honey
juice of 1/2 lemon
1 cinnamon stick
1 vanilla bean, split lengthwise
2-inch piece of pared orange zest
1 whole clove
1 black peppercorn
4 firm, ripe pears
low-fat plain yogurt, to serve (optional)
mint leaves, to decorate

SERVES 4

1 In a large saucepan combine the wine, sugar, honey, lemon juice, cinnamon, vanilla bean, orange zest, clove and peppercorn. Heat gently, stirring occasionally, until the sugar dissolves.

2 Meanwhile, peel the pears, leaving the cores and stems intact. Slice a small piece off the bottom of each pear so it will stand upright.

3 Gently place the pears in the wine mixture. Simmer uncovered for 20–35 minutes, until the pears are just tender.

4 With a slotted spoon, gently transfer the pears to a bowl. Continue to boil the poaching liquid until reduced by about half. Pour into a bowl and let cool.

5 Strain the cooled liquid over the pears. Chill for at least 3 hours.

6 Place the pears in serving dishes, spoon the liquid over and decorate with a mint leaf. Serve alone or with low-fat plain yogurt.

NUTRITIONAL NOTES

Per portion:

Calories	398
Fat, total	0.2g
Saturated fat	0g
Cholesterol	0mg
Fiber	3.3g

APPLE FOAM WITH BLACKBERRIES

—

**This lovely light dish is perfect if you crave a dessert, but don't want anything
too rich or too filling.**

INGREDIENTS
2 cups blackberries
2/3 cup unsweetened
apple juice
1 teaspoon powdered gelatin
1 tablespoon honey
2 egg whites

SERVES 4

1 Place the blackberries in a pan with
1/4 cup of the apple juice and heat gently
until the fruit is soft. Remove from the
heat, cool, then chill.

2 Sprinkle the gelatin over the remaining
apple juice in a small pan and stir over
low heat until dissolved. Stir in the honey.

3 Beat the egg whites until they hold stiff
peaks. Continue beating hard while
gradually pouring in the hot gelatin
mixture, until well mixed.

4 Quickly spoon the foam into rough
mounds on individual plates. Chill.
Serve with the blackberries and juice
spooned around.

NUTRITIONAL NOTES
Per portion:

Calories	49
Fat, total	0.2g
Saturated fat	0g
Cholesterol	0mg
Fiber	1.7g

SENSATIONAL STRAWBERRIES

—

**Strawberries release their finest flavors when moistened
with a sauce of raspberries and passion fruit.**

INGREDIENTS

*3 cups raspberries, fresh
or frozen*
3 tablespoons sugar
1 passion fruit
1 1/2 pounds small strawberries
dessert cookies, to serve (optional)

SERVES 4

1 Mix the raspberries and sugar in a
saucepan and heat gently until the
raspberries release their juices. Simmer
for 5 minutes. Let cool.

2 Cut the passion fruit in half and scoop
out the seeds and juice into a bowl.

3 Pour the raspberry mixture into a food
processor or blender, add the passion
fruit and blend to a smooth purée.

4 Press the purée through a fine nylon
sieve placed over a bowl, to remove
the seeds.

5 Fold the strawberries into the sauce,
then spoon into four stem glasses. Serve
with the dessert cookies, if you like,
but these will increase the fat content
of the dessert.

COOK'S TIP

Berries taste best at room temperature;
take them out of the refrigerator half an
hour before serving.

NUTRITIONAL NOTES

Per portion:

Calories	115
Fat, total	0.5g
Saturated fat	0g
Cholesterol	0mg
Fiber	4.2g

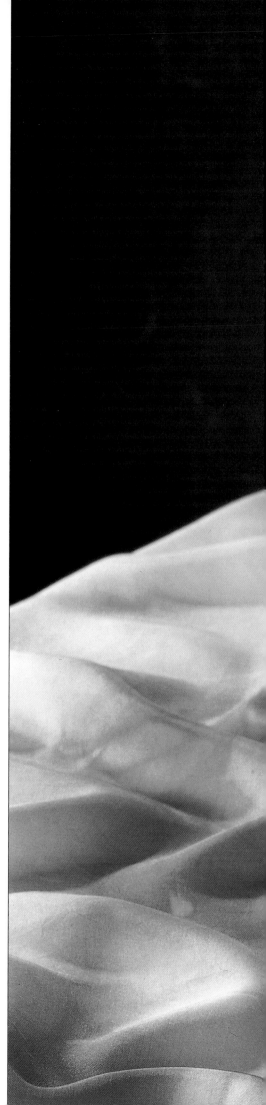

GREEK FIG AND HONEY PARFAIT

—

A quick and easy dessert made from fresh figs topped with yogurt, drizzled with honey and
sprinkled with pistachios.

1 Chop the figs and place in the bottom of
four stem glasses or deep, individual
dessert bowls.

2 Top each glass or bowl of figs with a
quarter of the yogurt. Chill until ready
to serve.

3 Just before serving drizzle 1 tablespoon
honey over each dessert and sprinkle with
the pistachios.

INGREDIENTS

4 fresh figs
2 cups low-fat plain yogurt
4 tablespoons honey
*2 teaspoons chopped, unsalted
pistachios*

SERVES 4

NUTRITIONAL NOTES
Per portion:

Calories	158
Fat, total	4.7g
Saturated fat	2.21g
Cholesterol	6.1mg
Fiber	0.8g

COOK'S TIP
Look out for specialty honeys made
from the nectar of flowers like
lavender, clover, acacia, heather,
rosemary and thyme.
If unsalted pistachios are difficult to
find, substitute chopped walnuts or
almonds instead.

FIGS WITH RICOTTA CREAM

Fresh, ripe figs are full of natural sweetness. This simple recipe makes the most of their beautiful, intense flavor.

INGREDIENTS
4 ripe, fresh figs
1/2 cup ricotta cheese
3 tablespoons reduced-fat crème fraîche
1 tablespoon honey
1/2 teaspoon pure vanilla extract
freshly grated nutmeg, to decorate

SERVES 4

COOK'S TIP
The honey can be omitted and replaced with a little artificial sweetener.

1 Using a small sharp knife, trim the stalks from the figs. Make four cuts through each fig from the stalk-end, cutting them almost through but being careful to leave them joined at the bottom.

2 Place the figs on serving plates and open them out.

3 In a bowl, mix together the ricotta cheese, crème fraîche, honey and vanilla extract.

4 Spoon a little ricotta cream mixture on to each plate and sprinkle with grated nutmeg to serve.

NUTRITIONAL NOTES
Per portion:

Calories	97
Fat, total	5.0g
Saturated fat	3.04g
Cholesterol	26.2mg
Fiber	0.8g

PASTRIES,
CAKES,
PIES AND
CRÊPES

These desserts will impress and provide a
stunning end to a special occasion or dinner party.
Irresistible cakes, light-as-air meringues and
fruit-filled crêpes make a spectacular finale.

SPICED MANGO PHYLLO TARTS

Mangoes have a wonderful texture and look great simply sliced and fanned out
next to these crunchy phyllo tarts.

INGREDIENTS
4 mangoes
6 phyllo pastry sheets
7 tablespoons butter, melted
3 tablespoons light brown sugar
4 teaspoons ground cinnamon
confectioners' sugar, for dusting

SERVES 8

1 Preheat the oven to 400°F. Set the most
perfect mango aside for the decoration.
Peel the remaining mangoes and slice the
flesh across into ⅛-inch thick slices.

2 Keeping the rest of the phyllo covered
with a damp dish towel, lay one sheet on
a baking sheet and brush with melted
butter. Mix the brown sugar and cinnamon
together and sprinkle one-fifth of the
mixture over the phyllo. Lay another
sheet of phyllo on top and repeat for the
other 5 sheets, ending with a phyllo sheet.

NUTRITIONAL NOTES
Per portion:

Calories	207
Fat, total	5.0g
Saturated fat	2.75g
Cholesterol	11.5mg
Fiber	3.6g

3 Brush the top phyllo sheet with butter,
trim off the excess pastry and lay the
sliced mango in neat rows across the
layered phyllo, to cover it completely.
Brush with the reserved butter and bake
for 30 minutes. Allow to cool on the
baking sheet, then cut into rectangles.

4 Slice the flesh from either side of the
pit of the reserved mango. Cut each piece
in half lengthwise. Make four long cuts,
almost to the end, in each quarter. Dust
with confectioners' sugar. Put on a plate
and carefully fan out the slices. Serve
with the mango tarts.

PHYLLO RHUBARB CHIFFON PIE

Phyllo pastry is low in fat and is very easy to bake. Keep a package in the freezer, ready to make impressive desserts like this one.

INGREDIENTS

1¼ pounds pink rhubarb

1 teaspoon apple pie spice

· finely grated zest and juice of 1 orange

1 tablespoon sugar

1 tablespoon low-fat spread

3 sheets phyllo pastry, thawed if frozen

SERVES 3

VARIATION

Other fruit such as apples, pears or peaches can be used in this pie—try it with whatever fruit is in season.

1 Preheat the oven to 400°F. Trim the leaves and ends from the rhubarb stalks and chop them into 1-inch pieces. Place them in a medium-sized mixing bowl.

2 Add the apple pie spice, orange zest and juice and sugar; toss well to coat evenly. Pour the rhubarb into a 4-cup pie pan.

3 Melt the spread and brush over the phyllo sheets. Crumple the phyllo loosely and place the pieces on top of the filling to cover.

4 Place the dish on a baking sheet and bake the pie for 20 minutes, until golden brown. Reduce the heat to 350°F and bake for 10–15 minutes more, until the rhubarb is tender. Serve warm.

NUTRITIONAL NOTES
Per portion:

Calories	118
Fat, total	3g
Saturated fat	0.65g
Cholesterol	0.3mg
Fiber	2.4g

APRICOT AND PEAR PHYLLO ROULADE

—

This is a very quick way of making a strudel—normally, a very time consuming task—
but it tastes delicious all the same!

INGREDIENTS

1/2 cup dried apricots, chopped
2 tablespoons apricot conserve
1 teaspoon lemon juice
1/3 cup light brown sugar
2 pears, peeled, cored and chopped
2 tablespoons flaked almonds
2 tablespoons low-fat spread, melted
8 sheets phyllo pastry, thawed if frozen
1 teaspoon confectioners' sugar,
for dusting

SERVES 6

1 Put the apricots, apricot conserve, lemon juice, brown sugar and pears into a pan and heat for 5–7 minutes.

2 Remove from heat and cool. Mix in the flaked almonds. Preheat the oven to 400°F. Melt the low-fat spread completely.

3 Lightly grease a baking sheet. Layer the pastry on the baking sheet, brushing each layer with the melted spread.

4 Spoon the filling down the phyllo, keeping it to one side of the center and within 1-inch of each end. Lift the other side of the pastry up by sliding a spatula underneath.

5 Fold this pastry over the filling, tucking the edge under. Seal the ends neatly and brush all over with spread again. Bake for 15–20 minutes, until golden. Dust with confectioners' sugar and serve hot, cut into diamonds.

NUTRITIONAL NOTES
Per portion:

Calories	190
Fat, total	4.1g
Saturated fat	0.54g
Cholesterol	0.1mg
Fiber	2.6g

APRICOT PARCELS

—

These little phyllo parcels contain a special apricot and mincemeat filling. A good way to use up
any mincemeat and marzipan that are left over from Christmas!

NUTRITIONAL NOTES
Per portion:

Calories	234
Fat, total	4.4g
Saturated fat	1.1g
Cholesterol	3.7mg
Fiber	1.5g

2 Place an apricot half, hollow up, in the center of each pastry star. Mix together the mincemeat, crushed ratafias and marzipan and spoon a little of the mixture into the hollow in each apricot.

3 Top with another apricot half, then bring the corners of each pastry together and squeeze to make a gathered purse.

4 Place the purses on a baking sheet and brush each with a little melted spread. Bake for 15–20 minutes, or until the pastry is golden and crisp. Lightly dust with confectioners' sugar to serve.

INGREDIENTS

12 ounces phyllo pastry, thawed if frozen
2 tablespoons low-fat spread, melted
8 apricots, halved and pitted
4 tablespoons deluxe mincemeat
12 ratafias, crushed
2 tablespoons grated marzipan,
chopped finely
confectioners' sugar, for dusting

SERVES 8

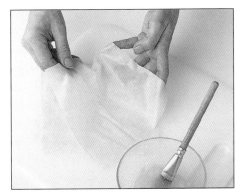

1 Preheat the oven to 400°F. Cut the phyllo into thirty-two 7-inch squares. Brush 4 of the squares with melted spread and stack them, giving each layer a quarter turn so that the stack acquires a star shape. Repeat to make 8 stars.

COOK'S TIP
If you have run out of mincemeat,
use mixed raisins instead.

PHYLLO FRUIT SCRUNCHIES

Quick and easy to make, these pastries are ideal to serve as an afternoon snack. Eat them warm
or they will lose their crispness.

INGREDIENTS

5 apricots or plums
4 sheets phyllo pastry, thawed if frozen
4 teaspoons low-fat spread, melted
1/3 cup demerara sugar
2 tablespoons flaked almonds
confectioners' sugar, for dusting

SERVES 6

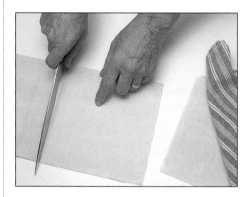

1 Preheat the oven to 375°F. Halve the
apricots or plums, remove the pits and
slice the fruit. Cut the phyllo pastry into
twelve 7-inch squares. Pile the squares
on top of each other and cover with a
clean dish towel to prevent the pastry
from drying out.

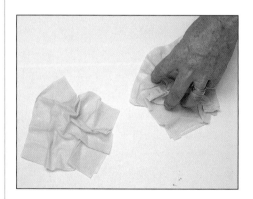

2 Remove one square of phyllo and brush
it with melted spread. Lay a second
phyllo square on top, then, using your
fingers, mold the pastry into folds.
Quickly make five more scrunchies in the
same way so that the pastry does not dry

3 Arrange a few slices of fruit in the folds
of each scrunchie, then sprinkle
generously with the demerara sugar and
flaked almonds.

4 Place the scrunchies on a baking sheet.
Bake for 8–10 minutes until golden brown,
then loosen the scrunchies from the
baking sheet with a spatula and transfer
to a wire rack. Dust with confectioners'
sugar and serve immediately.

NUTRITIONAL NOTES
Per portion:

Calories	132
Fat, total	4.19g
Saturated fat	0.63g
Cholesterol	0mg
Fiber	0.67g

PLUM PHYLLO POCKETS

—

**Cheese-filled plums, baked in phyllo pastry, provide a wonderful mix of
sweet and savory tastes for the palate.**

INGREDIENTS

1/2 cup low-fat soft cheese
1 tablespoon light brown sugar
1/2 teaspoon ground cloves
8 large, firm plums, halved and pitted
8 sheets phyllo pastry, thawed if frozen
sunflower oil, for brushing
confectioners' sugar, for dusting

SERVES 4

1 Preheat the oven to 425°F. Mix
together the low-fat soft cheese, brown
sugar and ground cloves to make a
firm paste.

2 Sandwich the plum halves together with
a spoonful of the cheese mixture. Stack
the phyllo pastry sheets and cut into
16 pieces, each 9-inches square. Brush
one piece with oil and place a second
diagonally on top. Repeat with the rest.

3 Place a plum on each phyllo pastry
square, lift up the sides and pinch the
corners together. Place on a baking sheet.
Bake for 15–18 minutes, until golden,
then dust with confectioners' sugar.

NUTRITIONAL NOTES
Per portion:

Calories	188
Fat, total	1.87g
Saturated fat	0.27g
Cholesterol	0.29mg
Fiber	2.55g

TROPICAL FRUIT PHYLLO CLUSTERS

These fruity phyllo clusters are ideal for a family treat or a dinner party dessert. They are
delicious served either hot or cold, on their own or with reduced-fat cream.

INGREDIENTS

1 banana, sliced
1 small mango, peeled, pitted and diced
lemon juice, for sprinkling
1 small cooking apple, coarsely grated
6 fresh or dried dates, pitted and chopped
⅓ cup dried pineapple,
chopped
⅓ cup golden raisins
⅓ cup light brown sugar
1 teaspoon ground apple pie spice
8 sheets phyllo pastry, thawed if frozen
2 tablespoons sunflower oil
confectioners' sugar, for dusting

SERVES 8

NUTRITIONAL NOTES

Per portion:

Calories	197
Fat, total	3.58g
Saturated fat	0.44g
Cholesterol	0mg
Fiber	2.31g

2 Add the apple, dates, pineapple, golden
raisins, sugar and spice to the bowl and
mix well.

3 To make each fruit cluster, cut each
sheet of phyllo pastry in half crosswise to
make two squares/rectangles (16 pieces
in total). Lightly brush two pieces of
pastry with oil and place one on top of
the other at a 45° angle.

4 Spoon some fruit filling into the center,
gather the pastry up over the filling and
secure with string. Place the cluster on
the prepared baking sheet and lightly
brush all over with oil.

5 Repeat with the remaining pastry
squares and filling to make a total of
8 fruit clusters. Bake for 25–30 minutes,
until golden brown and crisp.

1 Preheat the oven to 400°F. Line a
baking sheet with baking parchment.
In a medium-sized mixing bowl, toss
the banana slices and diced mango in
lemon juice to prevent discoloration.

COOK'S TIP

To prevent phyllo pastry drying out and
crumbling, cover with a damp cloth
before brushing with the oil.

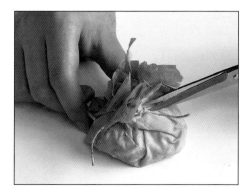

6 Carefully snip and remove the string
from each cluster and serve hot or cold,
dusted with sifted confectioners' sugar.

RED CURRANT PHYLLO BASKETS

Phyllo pastry is crisp and light and makes a very elegant dessert. It is also low in fat and needs
only a fine brushing of oil before use; a light oil such as sunflower is the best choice for this

INGREDIENTS

3 sheets phyllo pastry, thawed if frozen
1 tablespoon sunflower oil
1 1/2 cups red currants
1 cup low-fat plain yogurt
1 teaspoon confectioners' sugar

SERVES 6

1 Preheat the oven to 400°F. Cut the
sheets of phyllo pastry into eighteen
4-inch squares.

2 Brush each phyllo square very thinly
with oil, then arrange three squares in
each of six muffin pans, placing each one
at a different angle so that they form star-
shaped baskets. Bake for 6–8 minutes,
until crisp and golden. Lift the baskets
out carefully and let them cool on a
wire rack.

3 Set aside a few sprigs of red currants on
their stems for decoration and stem the
rest. Stir the red currants into the low-fat
plain yogurt.

4 Spoon the yogurt into the phyllo
baskets. Decorate them with the reserved
sprigs of red currants and sprinkle them
with the confectioners' sugar to serve.

NUTRITIONAL NOTES
Per portion:

Calories	80
Fat, total	3.8g
Saturated fat	1.35g
Cholesterol	2.3mg
Fiber	1g

PHYLLO FRUIT BASKETS

Crisp phyllo teamed with fruit in a strawberry yogurt cream makes a fine finish for a summer meal.

INGREDIENTS

4 large or 8 small sheets of phyllo pastry,
thawed if frozen
5 teaspoon low-fat spread, melted
1 cup low-fat plain yogurt
1/4 cup whole-fruit strawberry jam
1 tablespoon Curaçao or other
orange liqueur
1 cup seedless red grapes, halved
1 cup seedless green grapes, halved
1 cup fresh pineapple cubes
2 cups raspberries
2 tablespoons confectioners' sugar
6 small sprigs of fresh mint, for decorating

SERVES 6

1 Preheat the oven to 350°F. Grease 6 cups of a muffin pan.

2 Stack the phyllo sheets and cut into twenty-four 4½-inch squares.

NUTRITIONAL NOTES

Per portion:

Calories	207
Fat, total	4.6g
Saturated fat	1.84g
Cholesterol	3.2mg
Fiber	1.4g

3 Lay 4 squares of pastry in each of the 6 muffin pans. Press the phyllo firmly into the pans, rotating to make star-shaped baskets.

4 Brush the pastry baskets lightly with melted low-fat spread. Bake for 5–7 minutes, until the pastry is crisp and golden. Cool on a wire rack.

5 In a bowl, mix the yogurt with the strawberry jam and liqueur.

6 Just before serving, spoon a little of the cream mixture into each pastry basket. Top with the fruit. Sprinkle with confectioners' sugar and decorate each basket with a small sprig of mint.

PHYLLO-TOPPED APPLE PIE

—

With its scrunchy phyllo topping and only a small amount of low-fat spread, this makes a really light and healthy dessert.

INGREDIENTS

2 pounds cooking apples
6 tablespoons sugar
grated zest of 1 lemon
1 tablespoon lemon juice
1/2 cup golden raisins
1/2 teaspoon ground cinnamon
4 large sheets phyllo pastry, thawed if frozen
2 tablespoons low-fat spread, melted
confectioners' sugar, for dusting

1 Peel, core and dice the apples. Place them in a saucepan with the sugar and lemon zest. Drizzle the lemon juice over. Bring to a boil, stir well, then cook for 5 minutes or until the apples soften.

2 Stir in the golden raisins and cinnamon. Spoon the mixture into a 5-cup pie dish and level the top. Let cool.

NUTRITIONAL NOTES

Per portion:

Calories	199
Fat, total	2.5g
Saturated fat	0.56g
Cholesterol	0.3mg
Fiber	1.9g

3 Preheat the oven to 350°F. Place a pie funnel in the center of the fruit. Brush each sheet of phyllo with melted low-fat spread. Scrunch up loosely and place on the fruit to cover it completely.

4 Bake for 20–30 minutes until the phyllo is golden. Dust the pie with confectioners' sugar before serving.

VARIATION

To make phyllo crackers, cut the greased phyllo into 8-inch wide strips. Spoon a little of the filling along one end of each strip, leaving the sides clear. Roll up and twist the ends to make a cracker. Brush with more melted low-fat spread, bake for 20 minutes.

CHINESE CHESTNUT PANCAKES

Thin Chinese pancakes, spread with chestnut purée and sautéed in the minimum of oil, make a deliciously different dessert.

INGREDIENTS
3 ounces canned sweetened chestnut purée
1 tablespoon vegetable oil, for frying
sugar, to serve

FOR THE PANCAKES
1 1/4 cups all-purpose flour, plus
extra for dusting
about 7 tablespoons boiling water
1/2 teaspoon vegetable oil

SERVES 4

1 Make the pancakes. Sift the flour and then pour in the boiling water, stirring as you pour. Mix in the oil and knead the mixture into a dough. Cover with a damp towel and let stand for 30 minutes.

2 Knead the dough until smooth, then roll it out into a long "sausage", cut into eight pieces and roll each into a ball. Flatten each piece, then roll it to a 6-inch pancake.

NUTRITIONAL NOTES
Per portion:

Calories	192
Fat, total	3.8g
Saturated fat	0.47g
Cholesterol	0mg
Fiber	1.8g

3 Heat an ungreased frying pan until hot, then reduce the heat to low and place the pancakes, one at a time, in the pan. Turn them when small brown spots appear on the underside. Keep under a damp cloth until all are cooked.

4 Spread about 1 tablespoon of the chestnut purée over each pancake, then roll it up.

5 Heat the oil in a nonstick wok or frying pan. Add the rolls in batches and fry them briefly until golden brown, turning once.

6 Cut each pancake roll into three or four pieces and sprinkle with sugar. Serve immediately.

TROPICAL FRUIT CRÊPES

Fresh fruit, coated with a citrus and honey sauce, makes the perfect crêpe filling for this light and tasty dessert.

INGREDIENTS

1 cup self-rising flour
pinch of grated nutmeg
1 tablespoon sugar
1 egg
1¼ cups skim milk
1 tablespoon melted low-fat spread
1 tablespoon fine dried coconut (optional)
sunflower spray oil for frying
confectioners' sugar, for dusting
low-fat plain yogurt, to serve (optional)

FOR THE FILLING

8 ounces ripe, firm mango
2 bananas
2 kiwi fruit
1 large orange
1 tablespoon lemon juice
2 tablespoons unsweetened orange juice
1 tablespoon honey

SERVES 4

1 Sift the flour, nutmeg and sugar into a large bowl. In a separate bowl, beat the egg lightly, then beat in most of the milk. Add to the flour mixture and beat to make a thick, smooth batter. Add the remaining milk, melted spread and coconut, if using, and continue beating until the batter is smooth and of a fairly thin, dropping consistency.

NUTRITIONAL NOTES

Per portion:

Calories	303
Fat, total	4.7g
Saturated fat	0.98g
Cholesterol	49.9mg
Fiber	4.2g

2 Spray a large nonstick frying pan with a very thin coating of oil on to the surface. Heat, then pour in a little batter to cover the pan bottom. Fry until golden brown, then toss or turn with a spatula.

3 Repeat Step 2 with the remaining mixture to make about eight crêpes. Dice the mango, chop the bananas and slice the kiwi fruit. Peel the orange and cut into sections.

4 Place the fruit in a bowl. Mix the lemon and orange juices and honey, then pour over the fruit.

5 Spoon a little fruit down the center of a pancake and fold over each side. Repeat with the remaining crêpes, then dust with confectioners' sugar and serve alone or with low-fat plain yogurt.

BLUEBERRY PANCAKES

These fairly thick traditional pancakes were made popular as a breakfast option,
but they are equally good as a dessert for the whole family.

3 Heat a few drops of oil in a pancake pan or heavy frying pan until just hazy. Pour on about 2 tablespoons of the batter and swirl it around until it makes a neat pancake.

4 Cook for 2–3 minutes. When almost set on top, sprinkle 1–2 tablespoons of the blueberries over. As soon as the bottom is loose and golden brown, turn the pancake over.

5 Cook on the second side for only about 1 minute, until golden and crisp. Slide the pancake onto a plate and keep warm while you make 17 more pancakes in the same way. Serve drizzled with maple syrup, if you like, and offer lemon wedges for squeezing, if using.

INGREDIENTS

1 cup self-rising flour
pinch of salt
3 tablespoons sugar
2 eggs
1/2 cup skim milk
1 tablespoon vegetable oil
4 ounces fresh or frozen blueberries
maple syrup and miniature lemon wedges,
to serve (optional)

SERVES 6

1 Sift the flour and salt into a bowl. Add the sugar. In a separate bowl, beat the eggs thoroughly. Make a well in the middle of the flour and stir in the eggs.

2 Gradually blend in a little of the milk to make a smooth batter. Then whisk in the rest of the milk and continue to whisk for 1–2 minutes. Set aside for 20–30 minutes.

COOK'S TIP

Instead of blueberries you could use fresh or thawed and drained frozen blackberries or raspberries.

NUTRITIONAL NOTES
Per portion:

Calories	146/618kJ
Fat, total	3.9g
Saturated fat	0.76g
Cholesterol	64.6mg
Fiber	0.9g

APPLE AND BLACK CURRANT CRÊPES

These crêpes are made with a whole-wheat batter and are filled with a delicious fruit mixture.

3 Quarter, peel and core the apples. Slice them into a pan and add the black currants and water. Cook over gentle heat for 10–15 minutes, until the fruit is soft. Stir in enough demerara sugar to sweeten.

4 Apply a light, even coat of spray oil to a pan. Heat the pan, pour in about 2 tablespoons batter, swirl it around and cook for about 1 minute. Flip the crêpe over with a spatula and cook the other side. Keep the crêpe hot while cooking the remaining crêpes.

5 Fill the crêpes with the apple and black currant mixture and fold or roll them up. Serve with a dollop of crème fraîche, if using, and sprinkle with nuts or sesame seeds, if you like.

INGREDIENTS

1 cup whole-wheat flour
1¼ cups skim milk
1 egg, beaten
1 tablespoon sunflower oil
spray oil, for greasing
reduced-fat crème fraîche, to serve (optional)
toasted nuts or sesame seeds, for sprinkling (optional)

FOR THE FILLING

1 pound cooking apples
2 cups black currants
2–3 tablespoons water
2 tablespoons demerara sugar

SERVES 4

1 Make the crêpe batter. Place the flour in a mixing bowl and make a well in the center.

2 Add a little of the milk with the egg and the oil. Whisk the flour into the liquid, then gradually whisk in the rest of the milk, keeping the batter smooth. Cover the batter and put it in the refrigerator while you prepare the filling.

NUTRITIONAL NOTES
Per portion:

Calories	120
Fat, total	3g
Saturated fat	0.5g
Cholesterol	25mg
Fiber	0g

CHERRY CRÊPES

These crêpes are virtually fat-free, and lower in calories and higher in fiber than traditional ones. Serve with a spoonful of plain yogurt or low-fat fromage frais.

INGREDIENTS
1/2 cup all-purpose flour
1/2 cup whole-wheat flour
pinch of salt
1 egg white
2/3 cup skim milk
2/3 cup water
spray oil for frying

FOR THE FILLING
1 can (15 ounces) black cherries in syrup
1 1/2 teaspoons arrowroot

SERVES 4

1 Sift the flours and salt into a bowl, adding any bran left in the sieve to the bowl at the end. Make a well in the center of the flour and add the egg white, then the milk and water. Beat with a wooden spoon, gradually incorporating the surrounding flour mixture, then whisk the batter hard until it is smooth and bubbly.

2 Apply a light, even coat of spray oil to a nonstick frying pan. Heat the pan, then pour in a little batter to cover the bottom, swirling the pan to cover the bottom evenly.

3 Cook until the crêpe is set and golden, then turn to cook the other side. Slide onto paper towels and cook the remaining batter, to make 8 crêpes.

4 Drain the cherries, reserving the syrup. Mix about 2 tablespoons of the syrup with the arrowroot in a saucepan. Stir in the rest of the syrup. Heat gently, stirring, until the mixture boils, thickens and clears. Add the cherries and stir until thoroughly heated. Spoon the cherries into the crêpes and fold them in quarters. Serve immediately.

NUTRITIONAL NOTES
Per portion:

Calories	190
Fat, total	1.7g
Saturated fat	0.23g
Cholesterol	0.8mg
Fiber	2.2g

SUMMER BERRY CRÊPES

The delicate flavor of these fluffy crêpes contrasts beautifully
with tangy berries.

INGREDIENTS
1 cup self-rising flour
1 large egg
1 1/4 cups skim milk
a few drops of pure vanilla extract
spray oil, for greasing
confectioners' sugar, for dusting

FOR THE FRUIT
1 tablespoon low-fat spread
1/4 cup sugar
juice of 2 oranges
thinly pared zest of 1/2 orange
*3 cups mixed summer berries, such as
sliced strawberries, yellow raspberries,
blueberries and red currants*
*3 tablespoons Grand Marnier or other
orange-flavored liqueur*

SERVES 4

1 Preheat the oven to 300°F. To make the
crêpes, sift the flour into a large bowl and
make a well in the center. Break in the
egg and gradually whisk in the milk to
make a smooth batter. Stir in the vanilla
extract. Set the batter aside in a cool
place for up to half an hour.

2 Apply a light, even coat of spray oil to
an 7-inch nonstick frying pan. Whisk the
batter, then pour a little of it into the hot
pan, swirling to cover the bottom of the
pan evenly. Cook until the mixture comes
away from the sides and the crêpe is
golden underneath.

3 Flip the crêpe over with a large spatula
and cook the other side briefly until
golden. Slide the crêpe onto a heatproof
plate. Make seven more crêpes in the
same way. Cover the crêpes with foil or
another plate and keep them hot in a
warm oven.

COOK'S TIP
For safety, when igniting a mixture for
flambéing, use a long candle or long
wooden match. Stand back as you set
the mixture alight.

4 To prepare the fruit, melt the spread in
a heavy frying pan, stir in the sugar and
cook gently. Add the orange juice and
zest and cook until syrupy. Add the fruits
and warm through (keeping some back for
decoration), then add the liqueur and set
it aflame. Shake the pan until the flame
dies down.

5 Fold the crêpes into quarters and
arrange two on each plate. Spoon the fruit
mixture over and dust with confectioners'
sugar. Serve the remaining fruit separately.

NUTRITIONAL NOTES
Per portion:

Calories	285
Fat, total	5g
Saturated fat	1.06g
Cholesterol	59.5mg
Fiber	3.5g

BLUEBERRY AND ORANGE CRÊPE BASKETS

Impress your guests with these pretty, fruit-filled crêpes. When blueberries are out of season,
use other soft fruit, such as raspberries.

INGREDIENTS

1¼ cups all-purpose flour
pinch of salt
2 egg whites
scant 1 cup skim milk
⅔ cup orange juice
spray oil, for greasing

FOR THE FILLING

4 medium-size oranges
2 cups blueberries

SERVES 6

NUTRITIONAL NOTES

Per portion:

Calories	165
Fat, total	1.4g
Saturated fat	0.16g
Cholesterol	0.7mg
Fiber	3.2g

1 Preheat the oven to 400°F. Sift the flour and salt into a bowl. Make a well in the center and add the egg whites, milk and orange juice. Beat the liquid, gradually incorporating the surrounding flour mixture, then whisk the batter until it is smooth and bubbly.

2 Apply a light, even coat of spray oil to a heavy or nonstick pancake pan and heat it. Pour in just enough batter to cover the bottom of the pan, swirling it to cover the pan evenly.

3 Cook until the crêpe has set and is golden, and then turn it to cook on the other side. Slide the crêpe onto a sheet of paper towels. Cook the remaining batter, to make six crêpes.

4 Invert six small ovenproof bowls or molds on a baking sheet and drape a crêpe over each. Bake them in the oven for about 10 minutes, until they are crisp and set into shape. Carefully lift the "baskets" off the molds.

5 Pare a thin piece of orange zest from one orange and cut it in fine strips. Blanch the strips in boiling water for 30 seconds, rinse them in cold water and drain them on paper towels. Cut all the peel and white pith from all the oranges.

6 Cut the oranges into sections, working over a bowl to catch the juice. Add the sections and juice to the blueberries in a pan and warm gently. Spoon the fruit into the baskets and scatter the shreds of zest over the top.

COOK'S TIP
Don't fill the crêpe baskets until you are ready to serve them, because they will absorb the fruit juice and begin to soften.

BANANA, MAPLE AND LIME CRÊPES

Crêpes are a treat any day of the week, and they can be made in advance and
stored in the freezer for convenience.

INGREDIENTS
1 cup all-purpose flour
1 egg white
1 cup skim milk
¼ cup cold water
spray oil, for frying
shreds of lime zest, to decorate

FOR THE FILLING
4 bananas, sliced
3 tablespoons maple syrup or golden syrup
2 tablespoons fresh lime juice

SERVES 4

1 Make the crêpe batter by beating
together the flour, egg white, milk and
water in a bowl until smooth and bubbly.
Cover and chill until needed.

2 Apply a light, even coat of spray oil to a
nonstick frying pan. Heat the pan, then
pour in a little batter to coat the bottom.
Swirl it around the pan to coat evenly.

3 Cook the crêpe until golden, then toss
and cook the other side. Slide onto a
plate, cover with foil and keep hot while
making the remaining seven crêpes.

4 Make the filling. Mix the bananas,
syrup and lime juice in a pan and simmer
gently for 1 minute. Spoon into the crêpes
and fold into quarters. Sprinkle with
shreds of lime zest to decorate.

NUTRITIONAL NOTES
Per portion:

Calories	282
Fat, total	2.79g
Saturated fat	0.47g
Cholesterol	1.25mg
Fiber	2.12g

COOK'S TIP
Crêpes freeze well. To store for later
use, interleave them with nonstick
baking parchment, wrap and freeze for
up to 3 months.

PINEAPPLE AND STRAWBERRY MERINGUE

This is a gooey meringue that doesn't usually hold a perfect shape, but it has a
wonderful marshmallow texture.

INGREDIENTS

5 egg whites, at room temperature
pinch of salt
1 teaspoon cornstarch
1 tablespoon malt vinegar
few drops of pure vanilla extract
1¼ cups sugar
1 cup low-fat plain yogurt
6 ounces fresh pineapple, cut into chunks
1⅓ cups fresh strawberries,
halved
strawberry leaves, to decorate (optional)

SERVES 6

1 Preheat the oven to 325°F. Line
a baking sheet with nonstick
baking parchment.

2 Beat the egg whites in a large grease-
free bowl until they hold stiff peaks. Add
the salt, cornstarch, vinegar and vanilla
extract; beat again until stiff.

3 Gently beat in half the sugar, then
carefully fold in the rest. Spoon the
meringue onto the baking sheet and swirl
into a 8-inch round with the back of a
large spoon.

4 Bake for 20 minutes, then reduce the
oven temperature to 300°F and bake for
40 minutes more.

5 While still warm, transfer the meringue
to a serving plate, then let cool. To serve,
top with plain yogurt, pineapple chunks
and halved strawberries. Decorate with
strawberry leaves, if you have them.

NUTRITIONAL NOTES

Per portion:

Calories	247
Fat, total	2.2g
Saturated fat	1.31g
Cholesterol	2.9mg
Fiber	0.7g

COOK'S TIP

You can also cook this in a deep,
8-inch springform cake pan. Cover the
bottom with baking parchment
and grease the sides.

SOFT FRUIT PAVLOVA

—

There is rather a lot of sugar in meringue, but for special occasions this is the queen of desserts
and a practical way of using up leftover egg whites.

INGREDIENTS
oil, for oiling
4 egg whites
3/4 cup sugar
2 tablespoons red currant jelly
1 tablespoon rose water
1 1/4 cups low-fat
plain yogurt
4 cups mixed soft fruits, such as
blackberries, blueberries, red currants,
raspberries or loganberries
2 teaspoons sifted confectioners' sugar
pinch salt

SERVES 4

1 Preheat the oven to 275°F. Oil a baking
sheet. Beat the egg whites with a pinch of
salt in a spotlessly clean bowl, until they
are white and stiff. Slowly add the sugar
and keep beating until the mixture forms
stiff, glossy peaks.

NUTRITIONAL NOTES
Per portion:

Calories	302
Fat, total	3.9g
Saturated fat	2.37g
Cholesterol	5.3mg
Fiber	3.1g

2 Spoon the meringue into a 10-inch
round on the baking sheet, making a
slight indentation in the center and giving
it a swirled rim. Bake for 1–1 1/2 hours,
until the meringue is firm. Keep checking
as the meringue can easily overcook and
turn brown. Transfer the meringue to a
serving plate.

3 Melt the red currant jelly in a small
heatproof bowl resting in a pan of hot
water. Cool slightly, then spread the jelly
in the center of the meringue. Gently mix
the rose water with the low-fat plain
yogurt and spoon into the center of the
meringue. Arrange the fruits on top and
dust lightly with the confectioners' sugar.

HAZELNUT PAVLOVA

A hint of hazelnut gives the meringue a marvelous flavor, and provides a great contrast
to the summer fruit.

INGREDIENTS

3 egg whites

3/4 cup sugar

1 teaspoon cornstarch

1 teaspoon white wine vinegar

*3 tablespoons chopped
roasted hazelnuts*

1 cup low-fat soft cheese

1 tablespoon fresh orange juice

2 tablespoons low-fat plain yogurt

2 ripe nectarines, pitted and sliced

2 cups raspberries, halved

1 tablespoon red currant jelly, warmed

SERVES 4–6

1 Preheat the oven to 275°F. Lightly grease a baking sheet. Draw an 8-inch circle on a sheet of baking parchment. Place pencil-side down on the baking sheet.

2 Place the egg whites in a clean, grease-free bowl and beat until stiff. Add the sugar 1 tablespoon at a time, beating well after each addition.

3 Add the cornstarch, vinegar and hazelnuts and fold in carefully with a large metal spoon.

4 Spoon the meringue on to the marked circle and spread out to the edges, making a dip in the center.

5 Bake for about 1¼–1½ hours, until crisp. Let cool completely and transfer to a serving platter.

6 Beat the soft cheese and orange juice together, stir in the yogurt and spoon onto the meringue. Top with the fruit and drizzle the warmed red currant jelly over. Serve immediately.

NUTRITIONAL NOTES

Per portion:

Calories	332
Fat, total	4.4g
Saturated fat	0.82g
Cholesterol	0.3mg
Fiber	2.6g

NECTARINE AND HAZELNUT MERINGUES

—

If it's indulgence you're seeking, look no further. Sweet nectarines and yogurt paired with
crisp hazelnut meringues make a superb dessert.

INGREDIENTS

3 egg whites

3/4 cup sugar

1/2 cup chopped hazelnuts, toasted

1 1/4 cups low-fat

plain yogurt

1 tablespoon sweet dessert wine

2 nectarines, pitted and sliced

fresh mint sprigs, to decorate

SERVES 5

VARIATIONS

Use apricots instead of nectarines if
you prefer, or you could try this with a
raspberry topping.

1 Preheat the oven to 275°F. Line
two large baking sheets with baking
parchment. Beat the egg whites in a
grease-free bowl until they form stiff
peaks. Gradually beat in the sugar, a
spoonful at a time, until the mixture forms
a stiff, glossy meringue.

2 Fold in two thirds of the hazelnuts, then
spoon five large ovals onto each baking
sheet. Scatter the remaining hazelnuts
over five of the meringue ovals. Flatten
the remaining five ovals.

3 Bake the meringues for 1–1 1/4 hours,
until crisp and dry, then carefully lift
them off the baking parchment and cool
completely on a wire rack.

4 Mix the plain yogurt lightly with the
dessert wine. Spoon some of this mixture
onto each of the plain meringues. Arrange
a few nectarine slices on each. Put each
meringue on a dessert plate with a
hazelnut-topped meringue. Decorate each
portion with mint sprigs and serve the
meringues immediately.

NUTRITIONAL NOTES
Per portion:

Calories	293
Fat, total	4.9g
Saturated fat	2.34g
Cholesterol	4.2mg
Fiber	1.4g

BLACKBERRY-BROWN SUGAR MERINGUE

—

A brown sugar meringue looks very effective, especially when contrasted with a dark topping.

INGREDIENTS

1 cup light brown sugar
3 egg whites
1 teaspoon malt vinegar
1/2 teaspoon pure vanilla extract

FOR THE TOPPING

2 tablespoons crème de cassis
3 cups blackberries
1 tablespoon confectioners' sugar, sifted
1 1/4 cups low-fat
plain yogurt
small blackberry leaves, to decorate
(optional)

SERVES 6

1 Preheat the oven to 325°F. Draw an 8-inch circle on a sheet of baking parchment, turn over and place on a baking sheet.

2 Spread out the brown sugar on a second baking sheet and dry in the oven for 8–10 minutes. Sieve to remove lumps.

3 Beat the egg whites in a clean grease-free bowl until stiff. Add half the dried brown sugar, 1 tablespoon at a time, beating well after each addition. Add the vinegar and vanilla extract, then fold in the remaining sugar.

4 Spoon the meringue onto the circle, leaving a central hollow. Bake for 45 minutes, turn off the oven but leave the meringue in the oven with the door slightly open until cold.

5 Make the topping. In a bowl sprinkle crème de cassis over the blackberries. Let macerate for 30 minutes.

6 When the meringue is cold, carefully peel off the baking parchment and transfer the meringue to a serving plate. Stir the confectioners' sugar into the low-fat plain yogurt and spoon into the center.

7 Top with the blackberries and decorate with small blackberry leaves, if you like.

NUTRITIONAL NOTES

Per portion:

Calories	199
Fat, total	2.6g
Saturated fat	1.58g
Cholesterol	3.5mg
Fiber	1.8g

FLOATING ISLANDS IN HOT PLUM SAUCE

—

An unusual, low-fat dessert that is simpler to make than it looks. The plum sauce can be made in advance, and reheated just before you cook the meringues.

INGREDIENTS
1 pound red plums
1¹/4 cups unsweetened
apple juice
2 egg whites
2 tablespoons concentrated apple juice
freshly grated nutmeg

SERVES 4

1 Halve the plums and discard the pits. Place them in a wide pan with the unsweetened apple juice.

2 Bring to a boil, lower the heat, cover and simmer gently for 15–20 minutes, or until the plums are tender.

3 Meanwhile, place the egg whites in a grease-free bowl and beat them until they hold soft peaks.

4 Gradually beat in the concentrated apple juice, beating until the meringue holds fairly firm peaks.

5 Using a tablespoon, scoop the meringue mixture into the gently simmering plum sauce. You may need to cook the "islands" in two batches.

6 Cover and allow to simmer gently for 2–3 minutes, until the meringues are just set. Serve immediately, sprinkled with a little freshly grated nutmeg.

COOK'S TIP
A bottle of concentrated apple juice is a useful sweetener, but if you don't have any, use a little honey instead.

NUTRITIONAL NOTES
Per portion:

Calories	77
Fat, total	0.3g
Saturated fat	0g
Cholesterol	0mg
Fiber	1.7g

VARIATION
Add an extra dimension to this dessert by using a fruit liqueur such as Calvados, apricot brandy or Grand Marnier instead of the concentrated apple juice.

RASPBERRY VACHERIN

—

Meringue rounds filled with orange-flavored fromage frais and fresh raspberries
make a perfect dinner-party dessert.

INGREDIENTS

3 egg whites

3/4 cup sugar

1 teaspoon chopped almonds

confectioners' sugar, for dusting

raspberry leaves, to decorate (optional)

FOR THE FILLING

3/4 cup low-fat soft cheese

1 tablespoon honey

1 tablespoon Cointreau or other orange-flavored liqueur

1/2 cup low-fat fromage frais

2 cups raspberries

SERVES 6

1 Preheat the oven to 275°F. Draw an 8-inch circle on each of two pieces of baking parchment. Turn the paper over so the marking is on the underside and use it to line two heavy baking sheets.

NUTRITIONAL NOTES

Per portion:

Calories	248
Fat, total	2.22g
Saturated fat	0.82g
Cholesterol	4mg
Fiber	1.06g

2 Beat the egg whites in a grease-free bowl until very stiff, then gradually beat in the sugar to make a stiff meringue mixture.

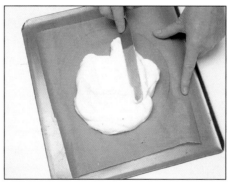

3 Spoon the mixture onto the circles on the prepared baking sheets, spreading the meringue evenly to the edges. Sprinkle one meringue round with the chopped almonds.

4 Bake for 1½–2 hours, then lift the meringue rounds off the baking sheets, peel away the paper and cool on a wire rack.

5 To make the filling, cream the soft cheese with the honey and liqueur in a bowl. Fold in the fromage frais and raspberries, reserving three of the best for decoration.

6 Place the plain meringue round on a board, carefully spread with the filling and top with the nut-covered round. Dust with confectioners' sugar, transfer to a serving plate and decorate with the reserved raspberries, and a sprig of raspberry leaves, if you like.

COOK'S TIP

When making the meringue, beat the egg whites until they are so stiff that you can turn the bowl upside-down without them falling out.

BAKED BLACKBERRY CHEESECAKE

—

This light, low-fat cheesecake is best made with wild blackberries, but cultivated ones will do;
or substitute other soft fruit, such as loganberries, raspberries or blueberries.

INGREDIENTS

low-fat spread, for greasing
³/4 cup low-fat cottage cheese
²/3 cup low-fat
plain yogurt
1 tablespoon whole-wheat flour
2 tablespoons turbinado sugar
1 egg
1 egg white
finely grated zest and juice of ¹/2 lemon
1³/4 cups fresh or thawed frozen
blackberries

SERVES 5

2 Place the cottage cheese in a food
processor and process until smooth.
Alternatively, rub it through a sieve,
to obtain a smooth mixture.

5 Run a knife around the edge of the
cheesecake, and then turn it out.
Remove the lining paper, and place the
cheesecake on a warm serving plate.

1 Preheat the oven to 350°F. Lightly
grease and line a 7-inch round cake pan.

3 Stir in the yogurt, flour, sugar, egg
and egg white. Add the lemon zest,
juice and blackberries, reserving a few
for decoration.

6 Decorate the cheesecake with the
reserved blackberries, and serve it warm.

4 Pour the mixture into the prepared pan
and bake it for 30–35 minutes, or until it
is just set. Turn off the oven and leave for
another 30 minutes.

COOK'S TIP

If fresh blackberries are not in season,
you can use canned blackberries.
Choose those canned in natural juice
and drain the fruit well before adding it
to the cheesecake mixture.

NUTRITIONAL NOTES

Per portion:

Calories	95
Fat, total	1.9g
Saturated fat	0.77g
Cholesterol	41.5mg
Fiber	1.4g

TOFU BERRY CHEESECAKE

This summery "cheesecake" makes a light and refreshing finish to any meal. Strictly speaking, it isn't a cheesecake at all, as it is based on tofu—but who would guess?

INGREDIENTS

FOR THE CRUST
2 tablespoons low-fat spread
2 tablespoons unsweetened apple juice
2 1/2 cups bran flakes or other high-fiber cereal

FOR THE FILLING
1 1/2 cups silken tofu
1 cup low-fat plain yogurt
1/4 cups apple juice
1 tablespoon powdered gelatin

FOR THE TOPPING
1 1/2 cups mixed summer soft fruit, such as strawberries, raspberries, red currants and blackberries
2 tablespoons red currant jelly
2 tablespoons hot water

SERVES 6

1 For the crust, place the low-fat spread and apple juice in a pan and heat them gently until the spread has melted. Crush the cereal and stir it into the pan, mixing well. Pour into a 9-inch round tart pan and press down firmly. Let set.

2 Make the filling. Place the tofu and yogurt in a food processor and process until smooth. Pour the apple juice into a cup and sprinkle the gelatin on top. Leave until softened, then place over hot water until melted. Stir quickly into the tofu mixture.

3 Spread the tofu mixture over the crust. Chill until set. Remove the tart pan and place the "cheesecake" on a serving plate.

4 Arrange the fruits over the top. Melt the red currant jelly with the hot water. Let it cool, then spoon over the fruit to serve.

NUTRITIONAL NOTES
Per portion:

Calories	163
Fat, total	4.4g
Saturated fat	0.93g
Cholesterol	1.6mg
Fiber	3.2g

ANGEL FOOD CAKE

**Serve this light-as-air cake with low-fat fromage frais—it makes a
perfect dessert or afternoon treat.**

3 Gently fold in the flour mixture with
a large metal spoon. Spoon into an
ungreased 10-inch angel food cake pan,
smooth the surface and bake for about
45–50 minutes, until the cake springs
back when lightly pressed.

4 Sprinkle a sheet of waxed paper with
sugar and set a bottle in the center. Invert
the cake pan over the paper, balancing it
carefully on the bottle. When cold, the
cake will drop out of the pan. Transfer it
to a plate, decorate if liked (see Cook's
Tip), then dust with confectioners' sugar
and serve.

INGREDIENTS

1/3 cup cornstarch
1/3 cup all-purpose flour
8 egg whites
*1 cup sugar, plus extra
for sprinkling*
1 teaspoon pure vanilla extract
confectioners' sugar, for dusting

SERVES 10

NUTRITIONAL NOTES

Per portion:

Calories	139
Fat, total	0.08g
Saturated fat	0.01g
Cholesterol	0mg
Fiber	0.13g

1 Preheat the oven to 350°F. Sift
both flours onto a sheet of waxed
paper.

2 Beat the egg whites in a large grease-
free bowl until very stiff, then gradually
add the sugar and vanilla extract, beating
until the mixture is thick and glossy.

COOK'S TIP

Make a lemony icing by mixing 1 1/2 cups
confectioners' sugar with 1–2 tablespoons
lemon juice. Drizzle over the cake and
decorate with Cape gooseberries.

CHOCOLATE AND ORANGE ANGEL FOOD CAKE

This light-as-air sponge with its fluffy icing is virtually fat free,
yet it tastes heavenly and looks great too.

INGREDIENTS

1/4 cup all-purpose flour
2 tablespoons low-fat
cocoa powder
2 tablespoons cornstarch
pinch of salt
5 egg whites
1/2 teaspoon cream of tartar
1/2 cup sugar
pared zest of 1 orange, blanched,
to decorate

FOR THE ICING

scant 1 cup sugar
5 tablespoons water
1 egg white

SERVES 10

2 Add the sugar to the egg whites a
spoonful at a time, beating for a few
minutes after each addition. Sift a third of
the flour and cocoa mixture over the
meringue and gently fold in with a
spatula. Repeat the procedure, sifting and
folding in the flour and cocoa mixture two
more times.

5 Beat the egg white in a grease-free
bowl until soft peaks occur. Add the
syrup in a thin stream, beating all the
time. Continue to beat until the mixture is
very thick and fluffy.

6 Spread the icing over the top and sides
of the cooled cake. Sprinkle the orange
zest over the top of the cake and serve.

1 Preheat the oven to 350°F. Sift the flour,
cocoa powder, cornstarch and salt
together three times. Beat the egg whites
in a large grease-free bowl until foamy.
Add the cream of tartar, then beat until
soft peaks form.

3 Spoon the mixture into a nonstick
8-inch ring mold and level the top. Bake
for 35 minutes or until springy when
lightly pressed. Turn upside-down onto a
wire rack and let cool in the pan.
Carefully lift off the pan.

4 Make the icing. Put the sugar in a pan
with the water. Stir over a low heat until
dissolved. Boil until the syrup reaches a
temperature of 250°F on a sugar
thermometer, or when a drop of the syrup
makes a soft ball when dropped into a
cup of cold water. Remove from heat.

COOK'S TIP

Make sure you do not over-beat the egg
whites. They should not be stiff but
should form soft peaks, so that the air
bubbles can expand during cooking.

NUTRITIONAL NOTES
Per portion:

Calories	153
Fat, total	0.27g
Saturated fat	0.13g
Cholesterol	0mg
Fiber	0.25g

CINNAMON APPLE GÂTEAU

—

**Make this lovely cake for an autumn celebration
when apples are at their best.**

INGREDIENTS

3 eggs
1/2 cup sugar
3/4 cup all-purpose flour
1 teaspoon ground cinnamon

FOR THE FILLING AND TOPPING

4 large eating apples
1/4 cup honey
1 tablespoon water
1/2 cup golden raisins
1/2 teaspoon ground cinnamon
1 1/2 cup low-fat soft cheese
1/4 cups low-fat fromage frais
2 teaspoons lemon juice
3 tablespoons smooth apricot jam, warmed
fresh mint sprigs, to decorate

SERVES 8

1 Preheat the oven to 375°F. Grease
and line a 9-inch round cake pan. Place
the eggs and sugar in a bowl and beat
until thick and mousse-like (when the
beater is lifted, a trail should remain on
the surface of the mixture for at least
15 seconds).

2 Sift the flour and cinnamon over the
egg mixture and carefully fold in with a
large spoon. Pour into the prepared pan
and bake for 25–30 minutes or until the
cake springs back when lightly pressed.
Slide a spatula between the cake and the
pan to loosen the edge, then turn the cake
onto a wire rack to cool.

3 To make the filling, peel, core and slice
three of the apples and put them in a
saucepan. Add 2 tablespoons of the honey
and the water. Cover and cook over a
gentle heat for about 10 minutes, until the
apples have softened. Add the golden
raisins and cinnamon, stir well, replace
the lid and let cool.

4 Put the soft cheese in a bowl with the
remaining honey, the fromage frais and
half the lemon juice. Beat until the
mixture is smooth.

5 Halve the cake horizontally, place the
bottom half on a board and drizzle any
liquid from the apple mixture over.
Spread with two-thirds of the cheese
mixture, then top with the apple filling.
Fit the top of the cake in place.

6 Swirl the remaining cheese mixture
over the top of the cake. Core and slice
the remaining apple, sprinkle with the
remaining lemon juice and use to decorate
the cake edge. Brush the apple with
apricot jam and decorate with mint sprigs.

NUTRITIONAL NOTES

Per portion:

Calories	244
Fat, total	4.05g
Saturated fat	1.71g
Cholesterol	77.95mg
Fiber	1.5g

PEACH JELLY ROLL

—

A feather-light sponge cake with a filling of peach jam—delicious as an afternoon snack or as a dinner-party dessert to impress your friends.

INGREDIENTS

low-fat spread, for greasing
3 eggs
1/2 cup sugar
3/4 cup all-purpose flour, sifted
1 tablespoon boiling water
6 tablespoons peach jam
confectioners' sugar, for dusting (optional)

SERVES 6–8

NUTRITIONAL NOTES

Per portion:

Calories	178
Fat, total	2.45g
Saturated fat	0.67g
Cholesterol	82.5mg
Fiber	0.33g

1 Preheat the oven to 400°F. Grease a 12 × 8-inch jelly roll pan and line with baking parchment. Combine the eggs and sugar in a bowl. Beat until thick and mousse-like (when the beater is lifted, a trail should remain on the surface of the mixture for at least 15 seconds).

2 Carefully fold in the flour with a large metal spoon, then add the boiling water in the same way.

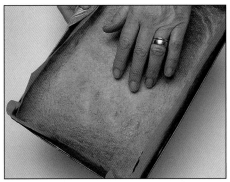

3 Spoon into the prepared pan, spread evenly to the edges and bake for about 10–12 minutes, until the cake springs back when lightly pressed.

4 Spread a sheet of waxed paper on a flat surface, sprinkle it with sugar, then invert the cake on top. Peel off the lining paper.

5 Neatly trim the edges of the cake. Make a neat cut two-thirds of the way through the cake, about 1/2-inch from the short edge nearest you.

6 Spread the cake with the peach jam and roll up quickly from the partially cut end. Hold in position for a minute, making sure the seam is underneath. Cool on a wire rack. Decorate with royal icing (see Cook's Tip) or simply dust with confectioners' sugar before serving.

COOK'S TIP

Decorate the jelly roll with royal icing. Put 4 ounces glacé icing in a piping bag fitted with a small writing nozzle and pipe lines over the top of the jelly roll.

APRICOT AND ORANGE ROULADE

—

This elegant dessert is very low in fat, so serving it with a spoonful of low-fat plain yogurt or fromage frais would not be disastrous.

INGREDIENTS
low-fat spread, for greasing
4 egg whites
1/2 cup turbinado sugar
1/2 cup all-purpose flour
finely grated zest of 1 small orange
3 tablespoons orange juice

FOR THE FILLING
1/2 cup dried apricots, roughly chopped
2/3 cup orange juice

TO DECORATE
2 teaspoons confectioners' sugar, for sprinkling
shreds of pared orange zest, to decorate

SERVES 6

1 Preheat the oven to 400°F. Grease a 9 × 13-inch jelly roll pan and line it with baking parchment. Grease the paper.

COOK'S TIP
Make and bake the sponge mixture a day in advance and keep it, rolled with the paper, in a cool place. Fill it with the fruit purée 2–3 hours before serving. The sponge can also be frozen for up to 2 months.

2 Place the egg whites in a large grease-free bowl and beat them until they hold soft peaks. Gradually add the sugar, beating hard after each addition.

3 Fold in the flour, orange zest and juice. Spoon the mixture into the prepared pan and spread it evenly.

4 Bake for 15-18 minutes, or until the sponge is firm and pale gold in color. Turn out onto a sheet of baking parchment, and roll it up loosely from one short side. Let cool.

5 Make the filling. Place the apricots in a pan with the orange juice. Cover the pan and let simmer until most of the liqud has been absorbed. Purée the apricots in a food processor.

6 Unroll the roulade and spread with the apricot mixture. Roll up, arrange strips of paper diagonally across the roll, sprinkle lightly with lines of confectioners' sugar, remove the paper and scatter with shreds of pared orange zest. Serve in slices.

NUTRITIONAL NOTES
Per portion:

Calories	154
Fat, total	0.3g
Saturated fat	0.01g
Cholesterol	0mg
Fiber	1.5g

LEMON CHIFFON CAKE

Lemon mousse provides a tangy filling for this light lemon sponge cake,
which is simple to prepare.

INGREDIENTS
low-fat spread, for greasing
2 eggs
6 tablespoons sugar
grated zest of 1 lemon
1/2 cup all-purpose flour, sifted
thinly pared lemon zest, cut in shreds

FOR THE FILLING
2 eggs, separated
6 tablespoons sugar
grated zest and juice of 1 lemon
2 tablespoons water
1 tablespoon powdered gelatin
1/2 cup low-fat fromage frais

FOR THE ICING
1 cup confectioners' sugar, sifted
1 tablespoon lemon juice

SERVES 8

1 Preheat the oven to 350°F. Grease and line an 8-inch springform cake pan. Beat the eggs, sugar and lemon zest until thick and mousse-like. Gently fold in the flour, then turn the mixture into the prepared pan.

2 Bake for 20–25 minutes until the cake springs back when lightly pressed in the center. Turn onto a wire rack to cool. Once cold, split the cake in half horizontally and return the lower half to the clean cake pan. Set aside.

3 Make the filling. Put the egg yolks, sugar, lemon zest and juice in a bowl. Beat with a hand-held electric beater until thick, pale and creamy.

4 Pour the water into a small heatproof bowel and sprinkle the gelatin on top. Set aside until spongy, then place over simmering water and stir until dissolved. Cool slightly, then beat into the yolk mixture. Fold in the fromage frais. When the mixture begins to set, quickly beat the egg whites to soft peaks. Fold a spoonful into the mousse mixture to lighten it, then fold in the rest.

5 Pour the lemon mousse over the sponge in the cake pan, spreading it to the edges. Set the second layer of sponge on top and chill until set.

6 Slide a spatula between the pan and the cake to loosen it, then transfer to a serving plate. Make the icing by adding enough lemon juice to the confectioners' sugar to make a mixture thick enough to coat the back of a wooden spoon. Pour over the cake and spread to the edges. Decorate with the lemon zest.

NUTRITIONAL NOTES
Per portion:

Calories	202
Fat, total	2.81g
Saturated fat	0.79g
Cholesterol	96.41mg
Fiber	0.2g

TIA MARIA GÂTEAU

A feather-light coffee sponge cake with a creamy liqueur-flavored filling
and a hint of ginger to give the flavor of the Caribbean.

INGREDIENTS

low-fat spread, for greasing
³/4 cup all-purpose flour
2 tablespoons instant coffee powder
3 eggs
¹/2 cup sugar
coffee beans, to decorate (optional)

FOR THE FILLING

³/4 cup low-fat soft cheese
1 tablespoon honey
1 tablespoon Tia Maria
¹/4 cup preserved ginger,
roughly chopped

FOR THE ICING

2 cups confectioners' sugar, sifted
2 teaspoons coffee extract
1 tablespoon water
1 teaspoon cocoa powder, preferably
reduced-fat

SERVES 8

1 Preheat the oven to 375°F. Grease
and line a 8-inch deep round cake pan.
Sift the flour and coffee powder together
onto a sheet of waxed paper.

2 Beat the eggs and sugar in a bowl until
thick and mousse-like (when the beater is
lifted, a trail should remain on the
mixture's surface for 10–15 seconds).

3 Gently fold in the flour mixture with a
metal spoon, being careful not to knock
out any air. Turn out the mixture into the
prepared pan. Bake the sponge for
30–35 minutes, or until it springs back
when lightly pressed. Turn out onto a wire
rack and let cool completely.

4 Make the filling. Mix the soft cheese
with the honey in a bowl. Beat until
smooth, then stir in the Tia Maria and
the chopped stem ginger.

5 Split the cake in half and sandwich the
two halves with the Tia Maria filling.

6 Make the icing. Mix the confectioners'
sugar and coffee extract with enough of
the water to make an icing that will coat
the back of a wood spoon. Spread three-
quarters of the icing over the cake. Stir
the cocoa into the remaining icing until
smooth. Spoon into a piping bag fitted
with a writing nozzle and pipe the mocha
icing over the coffee icing. Decorate with
coffee beans, if you like.

NUTRITIONAL NOTES

Per portion:

Calories	226
Fat, total	3.14g
Saturated fat	1.17g
Cholesterol	75.03mg
Fiber	0.64g

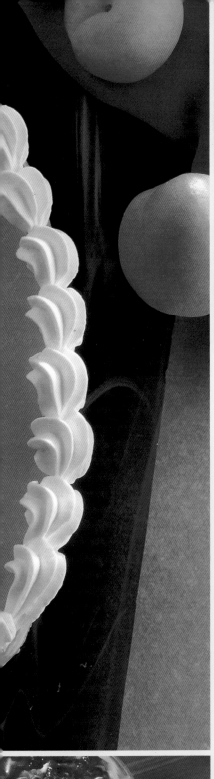

CUSTARDS, SOUFFLÉS AND MOUSSES

Creamy and light, yet satisfying and full of flavor,
these recipes are ideal to serve after a
rich main course to refresh the taste buds with
tantalizing flavors.

BREAD AND GOLDEN RAISIN CUSTARD

—

**An old favorite gets the low-fat treatment and proves
how successful it can be.**

INGREDIENTS

1 tablespoon low-fat spread
3 thin slices of bread, crusts removed
2 cups skim milk
1/2 teaspoon apple pie spice
3 tablespoons demerara sugar
2 eggs, beaten
1/2 cup golden raisins
freshly grated nutmeg
a little confectioners' sugar, for dusting

SERVES 4

1 Preheat the oven to 350°F and lightly grease an ovenproof dish. Spread the bread with low-fat spread and cut it into small pieces.

2 Place the bread in several layers in the prepared dish.

3 Beat together the skim milk, apple pie spice, demerara sugar and eggs in a large mixing bowl. Pour the mixture over the bread, covering it all. Sprinkle the raisins over and let stand for 30 minutes.

4 Grate a little nutmeg over the top and bake for 30–40 minutes, until the custard is just set and golden. Serve sprinkled with confectioners' sugar.

NUTRITIONAL NOTES

Per portion:

Calories	246
Fat, total	5g
Saturated fat	1.37g
Cholesterol	99.2mg
Fiber	0.7g

POPPYSEED CUSTARD WITH RED FRUIT

—

Poppyseeds add a nutty flavor to this creamy custard without increasing the amount of fat too much.

INGREDIENTS

low-fat spread, for greasing
2¹/2 cups skim milk
2 eggs
1 tablespoon sugar
1 tablespoon poppyseeds
1 cup each of strawberries, raspberries and blackberries
1 tablespoon light brown sugar
¹/4 cup red grape juice

SERVES 6

1 Preheat the oven to 300°F. Grease a soufflé dish very lightly with low-fat spread. Heat the milk until just below boiling point, but do not boil. Beat the eggs in a bowl with the sugar and poppyseeds until creamy.

2 Beat the milk into the egg mixture until very well mixed. Stand the prepared soufflé dish in a shallow roasting pan, then pour in hot water from the kettle to come halfway up the sides of the dish.

VARIATION

If you don't like poppyseeds, sprinkle the surface of the custard with freshly grated nutmeg or ground cinnamon instead.

3 Pour the custard into the soufflé dish and bake in the preheated oven for 50–60 minutes, until the custard is just set and golden on top.

4 While the custard is baking, mix the fruit with the sugar and fruit juice. Chill until ready to serve with the warm baked custard.

NUTRITIONAL NOTES

Per portion:

Calories	109Kcals
Fat, total	3.1g
Saturated fat	0.69g
Cholesterol	66.2mg
Fiber	1.3g

ORANGE YOGURT BRÛLÉES

—

Luxurious treats, much lower in fat than classic brûlées, which are made with cream, eggs and lots of sugar.

INGREDIENTS

2 oranges

2/3 cup low-fat
plain yogurt

1/4 cup reduced-fat crème fraîche

3 tablespoons turbinado sugar

2 tablespoons light brown sugar

SERVES 4

1 With a sharp knife, cut away all the peel and white pith from the oranges and chop the fruit. Or, if there's time, segment the oranges, removing all the membrane.

2 Place the fruit in the bottom of four individual flameproof dishes. Mix together the yogurt and crème fraîche and spoon the mixture over the oranges.

3 Mix together the two sugars and sprinkle them evenly over the tops of the dishes.

4 Place the dishes under a preheated, very hot broiler for 3–4 minutes, or until the sugar melts and turns to a rich golden brown. Serve warm or cold.

NUTRITIONAL NOTES

Per portion:

Calories	154/648kJ
Fat, total	3.8g
Saturated fat	2.35g
Cholesterol	15.8mg
Fiber	1.4g

TOFU BERRY BRÛLÉE

Brûlée is usually out-of-bounds on a low-fat diet, but this version is perfectly acceptable, because it uses tofu, which is low in fat and free from cholesterol.

INGREDIENTS
11-ounce package silken tofu
3 tablespoons confectioners' sugar
2 cups red berry fruits, such as raspberries,
strawberries and red currants
about 5 tablespoons demerara sugar

SERVES 4

NUTRITIONAL NOTES
Per portion:

Calories	180
Fat, total	3.01g
Saturated fat	0.41g
Cholesterol	0mg
Fiber	1.31g

1 Mix the tofu and confectioners' sugar in a food processor or blender and process until smooth.

COOK'S TIP
Choose silken tofu, which gives a smoother texture than firm tofu in this type of dish. Firm tofu is better for cooking in chunks.

2 Stir in the fruits, then spoon into a 3¾-cup flameproof dish. Flatten the top.

3 Sprinkle the top with enough demerara sugar to cover evenly. Place under a very hot broiler until the sugar melts and caramelizes. Chill before serving.

PASSION FRUIT BRÛLÉE

Fruit brûlées are usually made with heavy cream, but plain yogurt works very well. The brown
sugar required for this recipe is reserved for the crunchy caramelized topping.

INGREDIENTS

4 passion fruit

1¹/₄ cups low-fat

plain yogurt

¹/₂ cup light brown sugar

1 tablespoon water

SERVES 4

3 Put the sugar in a small saucepan with
the water and heat gently, stirring, until
the sugar has melted and caramelized.
Pour over the yogurt; the caramel will
harden within 1 minute. Keep the brûlées
in a cool place until ready to serve.

COOK'S TIP

Watch the caramel closely. It is ready
when it darkens to a rich golden brown.
At this stage it will be very hot, so
protect your hand and pour it with
great care.

1 Cut the passion fruit in half, using a
very sharp knife. Use a teaspoon to scoop
out all the pulp and seeds and divide
among four ovenproof ramekins.

2 Spoon equal amounts of the yogurt on
top of the fruit and smooth the surface
level. Chill for at least 2 hours.

NUTRITIONAL NOTES

Per portion:

Calories	139
Fat, total	3.8g
Saturated fat	2.37g
Cholesterol	5.3mg
Fiber	0.5g

MANGO AND GINGER CLOUDS

The sweet, perfumed flavor of ripe mango combines beautifully with ginger, and this low-fat
dessert makes the very most of both of them.

INGREDIENTS

3 ripe mangoes
3 pieces preserved ginger, plus 3
tablespoons syrup from the jar
1/2 cup silken tofu
3 egg whites
6 unsalted pistachios, chopped

SERVES 6

1 Cut the mangoes' flesh off the pit,
remove the peel and chop the flesh.

2 Put the mango flesh in a food processor
and add the ginger, syrup and tofu.
Process until smooth. Spoon into a bowl.

3 Beat the egg whites in a grease-free
bowl until they form soft peaks. Fold
them lightly into the mango mixture.

4 Spoon the mixture into wide dishes or
glasses and chill before serving,
sprinkled with the chopped pistachios.

NUTRITIONAL NOTES
Per portion:

Calories	141
Fat, total	1.9g
Saturated fat	0.21g
Cholesterol	0mg
Fiber	3.9g

NOTE
Raw or lightly cooked egg whites
should be avoided by women
during pregnancy.

RASPBERRY PASSION FRUIT SWIRLS

—

**If passion fruit is not available, this simple dessert can be made with
raspberries alone.**

2 Place alternate spoonfuls of the
raspberry pulp and the fromage frais
mixture into stem glasses or
serving dishes.

3 Stir lightly to create a swirled effect.
Decorate each dessert with a whole
raspberry and a sprig of fresh mint.
Serve chilled.

INGREDIENTS
2¹/2 cups raspberries
2 passion fruits
1²/3 cups low-fat
fromage frais
2 tablespoons sugar
raspberries and fresh mint sprigs,
to decorate

SERVES 4

COOK'S TIP
Over-ripe, slightly soft fruit can be
used in this recipe. Use frozen
raspberries when fresh are not
available, but thaw them first.

1 Using a fork, mash the raspberries in a
small bowl until the juice runs. Place the
fromage frais and sugar in a separate
bowl. Halve the passion fruit and scoop
out the seeds. Add to the fromage frais
and mix well.

NUTRITIONAL NOTES
Per portion:

Calories	110
Fat, total	0.47g
Saturated fat	0.13g
Cholesterol	1mg
Fiber	2.12g

CHOCOLATE VANILLA TIMBALES

You really can allow yourself the occasional chocolate treat, especially if
it's a dessert as light as this one.

INGREDIENTS

1¹/2 cups skim milk
2 tablespoons cocoa powder, plus extra
for sprinkling
2 eggs, separated
1 teaspoon pure vanilla extract
3 tablespoons sugar
1 tablespoon powdered gelatin
3 tablespoons hot water

FOR THE SAUCE

¹/2 cup low-fat plain yogurt
¹/2 teaspoon pure vanilla extract

SERVES 6

1 Mix the milk and cocoa in a pan; stir over moderate heat until the milk boils. Beat the egg yolks with the vanilla and sugar in a bowl, until smooth. Pour in the chocolate milk, beating well.

2 Return the mixture to the pan and stir constantly over gentle heat, without boiling, until it thickens slightly and is smooth. Dissolve the gelatin in the hot water and then quickly stir it into the milk mixture. Let it cool until the point of setting.

3 Beat the egg whites in a grease-free bowl until they hold soft peaks. Fold them quickly into the chocolate milk mixture, then divide among six individual molds. Chill until set.

4 To serve the timbales, run a knife around the edge of each mold, dip the molds quickly into hot water and turn out onto serving plates. For the sauce, stir the yogurt and vanilla extract together, then spoon onto the plates. Sprinkle the sauce with cocoa powder just before serving.

NUTRITIONAL NOTES

Per portion:

Calories	118
Fat, total	4.1g
Saturated fat	1.89g
Cholesterol	66.7mg
Fiber	0.7g

PEACH AND GINGER PASHKA

Another low-fat version of the Russian Easter favorite—this time with peaches
and preserved ginger.

INGREDIENTS

1¹/2 cups low-fat cottage cheese
2 ripe peaches or nectarines
scant ¹/2 cup low-fat
plain yogurt
2 pieces preserved ginger in syrup, drained
and chopped, plus 2 tablespoons syrup
from the jar
¹/2 teaspoon pure vanilla extract

TO DECORATE

1 peach or nectarine, peeled and sliced
2 teaspoons slivered almonds, toasted

SERVES 4

1 Drain the cottage cheese and rub it
through a sieve into a bowl. Pit and
roughly chop the peaches or nectarines.

2 In a bowl, mix together the chopped
peaches or nectarines, the low-fat
cottage cheese, yogurt, ginger, syrup and
vanilla extract.

3 Line a new, clean flower pot or a
strainer with a piece of clean, fine cloth
such as cheesecloth.

4 Pour in the cheese mixture, wrap over
the cloth and weight down. Leave over a
bowl in a cool place to drain overnight.
Unwrap the cloth and invert the pashka onto
a plate. Decorate with fruit and almonds.

NUTRITIONAL NOTES

Per portion:

Calories	147
Fat, total	2.9g
Saturated fat	0.89g
Cholesterol	5.3mg
Fiber	1.1g

COOK'S TIP

Rather than making one large pashka,
line four to six cups or ramekins with
the clean cloth or muslin and divide
the mixture among them.

STRAWBERRY ROSE-PETAL PASHKA

—

This lighter version of a traditional Russian dessert is ideal for dinner parties—make it a day or two in advance for best results.

INGREDIENTS

1½ cups low-fat cottage cheese
¾ cup low-fat
plain yogurt
2 tablespoons honey
½ teaspoon rose-water
2½ cups strawberries
handful of scented pink rose petals,
to decorate

SERVES 4

VARIATION

Use small porcelain heart-shaped molds with draining holes for a pretty alternative.

---

1 Drain any free liquid from the cottage cheese and placep the cheese in a sieve. Use a wooden spoon to rub it through the sieve into a bowl. Stir the yogurt, honey and rose-water into the cheese.

2 Roughly chop about half the strawberries and fold them into the cheese mixture.

3 Line a new, clean flowerpot or a sieve with fine cheesecloth and pour the cheese mixture in. Set aside to drain over a bowl for several hours, or overnight.

4 Invert the flowerpot or sieve onto a serving plate, turn out the pashka and lift off the cheesecloth. Cut the remaining strawberries in half and arrange them around the pashka. Scatter the rose petals over. Serve chilled.

NUTRITIONAL NOTES

Per portion:

Calories	133
Fat, total	1.6g
Saturated fat	1g
Cholesterol	6.1mg
Fiber	0.8g

LEMON HEARTS WITH STRAWBERRY SAUCE

These elegant little hearts are perfect for a romantic celebration, such as a
Valentine's Day dinner.

INGREDIENTS

3/4 cup low-fat cottage cheese
*2/3 cup reduced-fat
crème fraîche*
1 tablespoon granulated sugar
finely grated zest of 1/2 lemon
2 tablespoons lemon juice
2 teaspoons powder gelatin
2 egg whites
low-fat spread, for greasing

FOR THE SAUCE

*2 cups fresh or frozen and thawed
strawberries, plus extra to decorate*
1 tablespoon lemon juice

SERVES 6

1 Press the cottage cheese through a
sieve into a bowl. Beat in the crème
fraîche, sugar and lemon zest.

2 Pour the lemon juice into a small
heatproof bowl and sprinkle the gelatin
over the surface. When it has softened,
place the bowl over a pan of hot water and
stir to dissolve the gelatin completely.

3 Quickly stir the gelatin into the cheese
mixture, mixing it in evenly.

4 Beat the egg whites in a grease-free
bowl until they form soft peaks. Quickly
fold them into the cheese mixture.

5 Spoon the mixture into six lightly
greased, individual heart-shaped molds,
and chill the molds until set.

6 Make the sauce. Mix the strawberries
and lemon juice in a food processor or
blender and process until smooth. Pour
the sauce onto serving plates and invert
the lemon hearts on top. Decorate with
slices of strawberry.

COOK'S TIP

Don't worry if you haven't got heart-
shaped (coeur à la crème) molds.
Simply use individual fluted molds—or
even ordinary teacups.

NUTRITIONAL NOTES

Per portion:

Calories	94
Fat, total	4.2g
Saturated fat	2.60g
Cholesterol	27.7mg
Fiber	0.4g

SOUFFLÉED RICE PUDDING

The fluffy egg whites in this unusually light rice pudding make the portions seem much more
substantial, without adding lots of extra fat.

INGREDIENTS

1/3 cup short-grain
(pudding) rice
3 tablespoons honey
3 cups low-fat milk
1 vanilla bean or 1/2 teaspoon
vanilla extract
2 egg whites
1 teaspoon freshly grated nutmeg

SERVES 4

1 Place the rice, honey and milk in a
heavy or nonstick pan and bring the
milk to a boil. Add the vanilla bean,
if using.

2 Lower the heat, cover and simmer over
the lowest possible heat for approximately
1–1¼ hours, stirring occasionally to
prevent sticking, until most of the liquid
has been absorbed.

3 Remove the vanilla bean, or, if using
vanilla extract, add this to the rice
mixture now. Set the pan aside, so that
the mixture cools slightly. Preheat the
oven to 425°F.

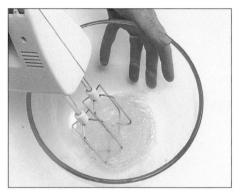

4 Place the egg whites in a grease-free
bowl and beat them until they hold soft
peaks when the beater is lifted.

5 Using a metal spoon or spatula, fold
the egg whites evenly into the rice
mixture, then pour it into a 4-cup
ovenproof dish.

6 Sprinkle with grated nutmeg and bake
for 15–20 minutes, until the pudding has
risen well and is golden brown. Serve hot.

NUTRITIONAL NOTES

Per portion:

Calories	186
Fat, total	3.7g
Saturated fat	1.88g
Cholesterol	13.1mg
Fiber	0g

COOK'S TIP

If you like, use skim milk instead of
low-fat, but take care when it is
simmering because, with so little fat, it
tends to boil over very easily.

CINNAMON AND APRICOT SOUFFLÉS

—

Don't expect this to be difficult simply because it's a soufflé—it really couldn't be easier, and, best of all, it's relatively low in fat.

INGREDIENTS
low-fat spread, for greasing
all-purpose flour, for dusting
3 eggs
1/2 cup apricot fruit spread
finely grated zest of 1/2 lemon
1 teaspoon ground cinnamon, plus extra to decorate

SERVES 4

NUTRITIONAL NOTES
Per portion:

Calories	134
Fat, total	4.1g
Saturated fat	1.15g
Cholesterol	144.4mg
Fiber	0g

1 Preheat the oven to 375°F. Lightly grease four individual soufflé dishes and dust them lightly with flour.

COOK'S TIP
Puréed fresh or well-drained canned fruit can be used instead of the apricot spread, but make sure that the mixture is not too wet or the soufflés will not rise properly.

2 Separate the eggs and place the yolks in a bowl with the fruit spread, lemon zest and cinnamon.

3 Beat hard until the mixture is thick and pale in color.

4 Place the egg whites in a grease-free bowl and beat them until they form soft peaks when the beater is lifted.

5 Using a metal spoon or spatula, gradually fold the egg whites evenly into the yolk mixture.

6 Divide the soufflé mixture among the prepared dishes and bake for 10–15 minutes, until well-risen and golden brown. Serve immediately, dusted with a little extra ground cinnamon.

VARIATION
Other fruit spreads would be delicious in this soufflé. Try peach or blueberry for a change.

FLUFFY BANANA AND PINEAPPLE SOUFFLÉ

—

This light, low-fat mousse looks very impressive but is really very easy to make,
especially with a food processor.

INGREDIENTS
2 ripe bananas
1 cup low-fat cottage cheese
1 can (15 ounces) pineapple chunks or
pieces in juice
¼ cup water
1 tablespoon powder gelatin
2 egg whites

SERVES 6

1 Tie a double band of baking parchment
around a 2½-cup soufflé dish, to come
approximately 2 inches above the rim.

2 Peel and chop one banana and place it
in a food processor with the cottage
cheese. Process the mixture until smooth.

3 Drain the pineapple and reserve a few
pieces for decoration. Add the rest of the
pineapple to the mixture in the processor
and process until finely chopped.

4 Pour the water into a small heatproof
bowl and sprinkle the gelatin on top.
Leave until softened, then place the bowl
over hot water, stirring occasionally, until
all the gelatin has dissolved.

5 Beat the egg whites in a grease-free
bowl until they hold soft peaks, then fold
them lightly and evenly into the mixture.
Pour the mixture into the prepared dish,
smooth the surface and chill it in the
refrigerator, until set.

6 When the soufflé has set, carefully
remove the paper collar. Decorate the
soufflé with the reserved slices of banana
and chunks of pineapple.

NUTRITIONAL NOTES
Per portion:

Calories	106
Fat, total	0.6g
Saturated fat	0.37g
Cholesterol	1.9mg
Fiber	0.7g

HOT BLACKBERRY AND APPLE SOUFFLÉS

—

**As the blackberry season is so short and the apple season so long, it's always worth freezing a
bag of blackberries to have on hand for treats like this one.**

3 Put a spoonful of the fruit purée into
each prepared dish and smooth the
surface. Set the dishes aside.

4 Beat the egg whites in a large grease-
free bowl until they form stiff peaks. Very
gradually beat in the remaining sugar to
make a stiff, glossy meringue mixture.

5 Fold in the remaining fruit purée and
spoon the flavored meringue into the
prepared dishes. Level the tops with a
spatula, and run a table knife around the
edge of each dish.

6 Place the dishes on the hot baking
sheet and bake for 10–15 minutes, until
the soufflés have risen well and are lightly
browned. Dust the tops with confectioners'
sugar and serve immediately.

INGREDIENTS

low-fat spread, for greasing
2/3 cup sugar, plus
extra for dusting
3 cups blackberries
1 large cooking apple, peeled, cored and
finely diced
grated zest and juice of 1 orange
3 egg whites
confectioners' sugar, for dusting

SERVES 6

1 Preheat the oven to 400°F. Grease six
2/3-cup soufflé dishes and dust with sugar.
Put a baking sheet in the oven to heat.

2 Cook the blackberries and diced apple
with the orange zest and juice in a pan for
10 minutes. Press through a sieve into a
bowl. Stir in 1/4 cup of the sugar. Set
aside to cool.

COOK'S TIP

Running a table knife around the edge
of the soufflés before baking helps
them to rise evenly without any part
sticking to the rim of the dishes.

NUTRITIONAL NOTES
Per portion:

Calories	138
Fat, total	0.3g
Saturated fat	0.5g
Cholesterol	0mg
Fiber	2.7g

SOUFFLÉED ORANGE SEMOLINA

Treat yourself to a taste of this sophisticated version.

INGREDIENTS
¹/4 cup semolina
2¹/2 cups low-fat milk
2 tablespoons brown sugar
1 large orange
1 egg white

SERVES 4

NUTRITIONAL NOTES
Per portion:

Calories	158
Fat, total	2.67g
Saturated fat	1.54g
Cholesterol	10.5mg
Fiber	0.86g

1 Preheat the oven to 400°F. Put the semolina in a nonstick pan and add the milk and sugar. Stir over moderate heat until thickened and smooth. Remove from heat.

COOK'S TIP
When using the zest of citrus fruit, scrub the fruit thoroughly before use, or buy unwaxed fruit.

2 Scrub the orange zest and pare a few long shreds of zest and save for decoration. Finely grate the remaining zest. Cut all the peel and white pith from the orange and separate the flesh into equal sections. Stir the sections into the semolina, with the orange zest.

3 Beat the egg white in a grease-free bowl until stiff but not dry, then fold lightly and evenly into the mixture. Spoon into a 4-cup ovenproof dish and bake for 15–20 minutes, until risen and golden brown. Scatter over the orange shreds and serve immediately.

QUICK APRICOT BLENDER MOUSSE

One of the quickest desserts you could make—and also one of the prettiest,
with its delicate swirl of creamy apricot.

INGREDIENTS

1 can (14 ounces) apricot halves in juice
1 tablespoon Grand Marnier or brandy
3/4 cup low-fat plain yogurt
1 tablespoon flaked almonds

SERVES 4

3 Alternately spoon fruit purée and yogurt into four tall glasses or glass dishes, swirling them together slightly to give a marbled effect.

4 Lightly toast the almonds until they are golden. Let them cool slightly and then sprinkle them on top of each mousse. Serve immediately.

1 Drain the juice from the apricots and place the fruit and liqueur in a blender or food processor.

2 Process the apricots until smooth.

NUTRITIONAL NOTES

Per portion:

Calories	88
Fat, total	4.4g
Saturated fat	1.38g
Cholesterol	3.1mg
Fiber	0.9g

PRUNE AND ORANGE CUPS

A simple, pantry dessert, made in minutes. It can be served immediately, but it is best chilled for
about half an hour before serving.

INGREDIENTS

1¹/2 cups dried prunes
²/3 cup orange juice
1 cup low-fat plain yogurt
shreds of thinly pared orange zest,
to decorate

SERVES 4

2 Bring the juice to a boil, stirring.
Lower the heat, cover and simmer for
5 minutes, until the prunes are tender
and the liquid is reduced by half.

5 Spoon the mixture into stem
glasses or individual serving dishes,
smoothing the tops.

1 Remove the pits (if any), then roughly
chop the prunes. Place them
in a pan with the orange juice.

3 Remove from heat, allow to cool
slightly, then beat well with a wooden
spoon, until the fruit breaks down to a
rough purée.

6 Top each pot with a few shreds of thinly
pared orange zest, to decorate. Chill
before serving.

COOK'S TIP

This dessert can also be made with
other dried fruit, such as apricots or
peaches. If using dried apricots, try
the unsulphured variety for a rich
color and flavor. For a special occasion,
add a dash of brandy or Cointreau
with the yogurt.

4 Transfer the mixture to a bowl. Stir in
the yogurt, swirling the yogurt and fruit
purée together lightly, to give an
attractive marbled effect.

NUTRITIONAL NOTES
Per portion:

Calories	125
Fat, total	0.7g
Saturated fat	0.28g
Cholesterol	2.3mg
Fiber	3.2g

GOOSEBERRY CHEESE COOLER

Gooseberries are one of the less common summer fruits, so they're well worth buying
when you can get them.

INGREDIENTS

4 cups fresh or frozen
gooseberries
1 small orange
1 tablespoon honey
1 cup low-fat cottage cheese

SERVES 4

NUTRITIONAL NOTES

Per portion:

Calories	93
Fat, total	1.4g
Saturated fat	0.56g
Cholesterol	3.1mg
Fiber	3.4g

1 Clean the gooseberries and place them
in a medium-sized saucepan. Finely grate
the zest from the orange and squeeze out
all of the juice; then add the orange zest
and juice to the pan. Cover the pan and
cook gently, stirring occasionally, until
the fruit is completely tender.

2 Remove from heat and stir in the
honey. Purée the gooseberries with the
cooking liquid in a food processor until
almost smooth. Cool.

3 Press the cottage cheese through a
sieve, or process it in a food processor,
until smooth. Stir half the cooled
gooseberry purée into the cheese.

4 Spoon the cheese mixture into four
serving dishes or glasses. Top each
with a spoonful of the gooseberry purée.
Serve chilled.

GRAPE CHEESE MOUSSE

—

A deliciously cool dessert of low-fat cheese and honey, topped with
sugar-frosted grapes as decoration.

INGREDIENTS

1¹/4 cups red or green seedless grapes, plus
tiny bunches
2 egg whites
1 tablespoon sugar
finely grated zest and juice of ¹/2 lemon
1 cup low-fat soft cheese
3 tablespoons honey
2 tablespoons brandy (optional)

SERVES 4

NUTRITIONAL NOTES

Per portion:

Calories	135
Fat, total	3g
Saturated fat	1.2g
Cholesterol	0.56mg
Fiber	0g

1 Brush the tiny bunches of grapes
lightly with egg white and sprinkle with
sugar to coat. Let dry.

2 In a bowl, mix together the lemon zest
and juice, cheese, honey and brandy if
using. Chop the remaining grapes and stir
them into the mixture.

3 Beat the egg whites in a grease-free
bowl until stiff enough to hold soft peaks.
Fold the whites into the grape mixture,
then spoon into serving glasses.

4 Top with the sugar-frosted grapes and
serve chilled.

APRICOT DELIGHT

—

A fluffy mousse base with a layer of fruit jelly on top makes this dessert doubly delicious.

INGREDIENTS

*2 cans (14 ounces each) apricots
in natural juice
¼ cup fructose
1 tablespoon lemon juice
1½ tablespoons powdered gelatin
15 ounces low-fat custard
⅔ cup low-fat plain yogurt,
strained*

TO DECORATE

*1 quantity yogurt piping cream
(see page 18)
1 apricot, sliced
1 sprig of fresh mint*

1 Line the bottom of a 5-cup heart-shaped or round cake pan with baking parchment.

COOK'S TIP

Don't use a loose-bottomed cake pan for this recipe as the mixture may seep through before it sets.

2 Drain the apricots, reserving the juice. Put the drained apricots in a food processor or blender. Add the fructose and ¼ cup of the apricot juice. Blend to a smooth purée.

3 Measure 2 tablespoons of the apricot juice into a small bowl. Add the lemon juice, then sprinkle 2 teaspoons of the gelatin over. Set aside for 5 minutes, until softened.

4 Stir the gelatin into half the apricot purée and pour into the pan. Chill in the refrigerator for 1½ hours, or until firm.

5 Sprinkle the remaining 1 tablespoon gelatin over ¼ cup of the apricot juice. Soak and dissolve as before. Mix the remaining apricot purée with the custard, yogurt and gelatin. Pour onto the layer of set fruit purée and chill in the refrigerator for 3 hours.

6 Dip the cake pan into hot water for a few seconds and unmold the heart onto a serving plate. Decorate with yogurt piping cream, the sliced apricot and a sprig of fresh mint.

NUTRITIONAL NOTES

Per portion:

Calories	155
Fat, total	0.63g
Saturated fat	0.33g
Cholesterol	0mg
Fiber	0.9g

FRUIT SALADS, ICES AND SORBETS

Cool, fresh and colorful—these wonderful combinations of textures and flavors make perfect desserts to follow spicy foods or simply to eat on a hot, sunny afternoon.

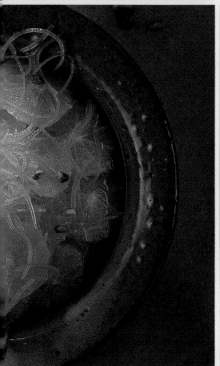

STRAWBERRIES WITH COINTREAU

—

Strawberries at the height of their season are one of summer's greatest pleasures. Try this simple but unusual way of serving them.

INGREDIENTS

1 orange

3 tablespooons sugar

5 tablespooons water

3¹/2 cups strawberries, hulled

3 tablespooons Cointreau or other orange-flavored liqueur

1 cup low-fat plain yogurt

SERVES 4

3 Reserve four strawberries for decoration and cut the rest lengthwise in halves or quarters. Put them in a bowl. Stir the Cointreau or chosen liqueur into the syrup and pour it over the fruit. Add the orange zest. Set aside for at least 30 minutes or for up to 2 hours.

NUTRITIONAL NOTES

Per portion:

Calories	155
Fat, total	3.2g
Saturated fat	1.97g
Cholesterol	4.4mg
Fiber	1.2g

4 Beat the yogurt briefly, then sweeten to taste with a little of the strawberry syrup.

5 Spoon the chopped strawberries into glass serving dishes and top with dollops of the sweetened plain yogurt. Decorate with the reserved strawberries.

1 With a vegetable peeler, remove wide strips of rind from the orange, taking care to avoid the pith. Stack two or three strips at a time and cut into very thin julienne strips.

2 Mix the sugar and water in a small saucepan. Heat gently, swirling the pan occasionally until the sugar has dissolved. Bring to a boil, add the julienne strips, then simmer for 10 minutes. Remove the pan from heat and let the syrup to cool completely.

FRESH FIGS WITH HONEY AND WINE

Fresh figs are naturally sweet, and they taste wonderful in a honeyed wine syrup.
Any variety can be used in this recipe, their ripeness determining the cooking time.

INGREDIENTS

scant 2 cups dry white wine

1/3 cup honey

1/4 cup sugar

1 small orange

8 whole cloves

1 pound fresh figs

1 cinnamon stick

bay leaves, to decorate

FOR THE SAUCE

1 1/4 cups low-fat
plain yogurt

1 teaspoon pure vanilla extract

1 teaspoon sugar

SERVES 6

1 Put the wine, honey and sugar in a heavy saucepan and heat gently until the sugar dissolves.

2 Stud the orange with the cloves and add to the syrup with the figs and cinnamon. Cover and simmer until the figs are soft. Transfer to a serving dish and cool.

3 Flavor the low-fat plain yogurt with the vanilla extract and sugar. Spoon it into a serving dish. With a small, sharp knife cut one or two of the figs in half, if you like, to show off their pretty centers. Decorate with the bay leaves and serve with the yogurt.

NUTRITIONAL NOTES
Per portion:

Calories	201
Fat, total	2.7g
Saturated fat	1.58g
Cholesterol	3.5mg
Fiber	1.5g

PERSIAN MELON CUPS

This typical Persian dessert uses delicious, sweet fresh fruits flavored with rose-water
and a hint of aromatic mint.

2 Reserve four strawberries and slice the rest. Place in a bowl with the melon balls, the peaches, grapes, sugar, rose-water and lemon juice.

3 Pile the fruit into the melon shells and chill in the refrigerator for 2 hours.

4 To serve, sprinkle with crushed ice and decorate each melon shell with a whole strawberry and a sprig of mint.

INGREDIENTS
2 small melons
2 cups strawberries, sliced
3 peaches, peeled and cut into small cubes
1 bunch of seedless grapes, about 8 ounces
2 tablespoons sugar
1 tablespoon rose-water
1 tablespoon lemon juice
crushed ice
4 sprigs of mint, to decorate

SERVES 4

1 Carefully cut the melons in half and remove the seeds. Scoop out the flesh with a melon baller, taking care not to damage the skin. Reserve the melon shells for later.

COOK'S TIP
If you don't have a melon baller, scoop out the melon flesh using a large spoon and cut into bite-size pieces.

NUTRITIONAL NOTES
Per portion:

Calories	137
Fat, total	0.4g
Saturated fat	0g
Cholesterol	0mg
Fiber	3.2g

FRAGRANT MANDARINS WITH PISTACHIOS

Mandarins, tangerines, clementines, mineolas: any of these lovely citrus fruits could be used for this dessert.

INGREDIENTS

10 mandarins
1 tablespoon confectioners' sugar
2 tablespoons orange-flower water
1 tablespoon chopped pistachios

SERVES 4

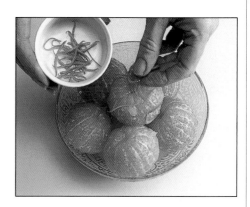

3 Mix the mandarin juice, confectioners' sugar and orange-flower water and pour it over the fruit. Cover the dish and place in the refrigerator for at least an hour to chill.

4 Blanch the shreds of mandarin zest in boiling water for 30 seconds. Drain and cool on paper towels, then sprinkle them over the mandarins, with the pistachios, to serve.

1 Pare a little of the mandarin zest and cut into fine shreds. Squeeze the juice from two mandarins and set it aside.

2 Peel the remaining fruit, removing all pith. Arrange the whole fruit in a wide dish.

NUTRITIONAL NOTES

Per portion:

Calories	91
Fat, total	2.2g
Saturated fat	0.25g
Cholesterol	0mg
Fiber	2g

ORANGE AND DATE SALAD

This Moroccan dessert using ingredients popular in North Africa is simplicity itself,
yet it is wonderfully refreshing and light at the end of a rich meal.

INGREDIENTS

6 oranges
*1–2 tablespoons orange-flower water or
rose-water (optional)*
lemon juice (optional)
2/3 cup pitted dates
scant 1/2 cup pistachios
*1 tablespoon confectioners' sugar,
plus extra for dusting*
1 teaspoon toasted almonds

SERVES 6

1 Peel the oranges with a sharp knife, removing all the pith. Cut into sections, catching the juice in a bowl. Place in a serving dish.

2 Stir in the juice from the bowl, with a little orange-flower or rose-water, if using, and sharpen with lemon juice, if you like.

3 Chop the dates and pistachios and sprinkle over the salad with the confectioners' sugar. Chill for 1 hour.

4 Just before serving, sprinkle the salad with the toasted almonds and a little extra confectioners' sugar.

NUTRITIONAL NOTES
Per portion:

Calories	147
Fat, total	4.3g
Saturated fat	0.45g
Cholesterol	0mg
Fiber	3.5g

COOK'S TIP
Use fresh dates, if you can, although if you can't get hold of them dried dates are delicious in this salad, too.

FRESH FRUIT SALAD AND ALMOND JELLY

Also known as Almond Float, this is a wonderfully light Chinese dessert usually made from agar-agar or isinglass, though gelatin can also be used.

2 In a separate saucepan, dissolve the sugar in the remaining water over the heat. Add the milk and the almond extract. Blend well, but do not boil.

3 Pour the agar-agar or gelatin mixture into a large serving bowl. Add the flavored milk gradually, stirring all the time. When cool, put in the refrigerator for 2–3 hours to set. To serve, cut the jelly into small cubes and spoon into a serving dish or into individual bowls. Spoon the fruit salad over the jelly and serve.

INGREDIENTS

¹/4 ounce agar-agar or Kanten flakes or
1 ounce gelatin
about 2¹/2 cups water
¹/4 cup sugar
1¹/4 cups low-fat milk
1 teaspoon pure almond extract
fresh fruit salad

SERVES 6

1 In a saucepan, dissolve the agar-agar in about half of the water over gentle heat. This will take at least 10 minutes. If using gelatin, follow the instructions on the envelope.

NUTRITIONAL NOTES
Per portion:

Calories	117
Fat, total	1.2g
Saturated fat	0.75g
Cholesterol	5.3mg
Fiber	0g

FRESH PINEAPPLE WITH COCONUT

This refreshing dessert can also be made with vacuum-packed pineapple,
and it is very simple to make and light to eat.

INGREDIENTS

1 fresh pineapple, about
1¹/2 pounds, peeled
few slivers of fresh coconut
1¹/4 cups unsweetened pineapple juice
¹/4 cup coconut liqueur
1-inch piece preserved ginger, plus
3 tablespoons syrup from the jar

SERVES 4

3 Thinly slice the preserved ginger and
add to the pan with the ginger syrup.
Bring just to a boil, then simmer gently
until the liquid is slightly reduced and
the sauce is fairly thick.

4 Pour the sauce over the pineapple and
coconut, let cool, then chill in the
refrigerator before serving.

1 Peel and slice the pineapple, arrange in
a serving dish and scatter the coconut
slivers on top.

2 Place the pineapple juice and coconut
liqueur in a saucepan and heat gently.

NUTRITIONAL NOTES

Per portion:

Calories	177
Fat, total	2.2g
Saturated fat	1.55g
Cholesterol	0mg
Fiber	2.2g

PERFUMED PINEAPPLE SALAD

This refreshing fruit salad benefits from being prepared ahead. This gives the fruit time to
absorb the perfumed flavor of the orange-flower water.

INGREDIENTS
1 small ripe pineapple
1 tablespoon confectioners' sugar
1 tablespoon orange-flower water, or
more if liked
2/3 cup fresh dates, pitted
and quartered
2 cups fresh strawberries, sliced
a few fresh mint sprigs, to serve

SERVES 4

1 Cut the skin from the pineapple and,
using the tip of a vegetable peeler,
remove as many brown "eyes" as possible.
Quarter the pineapple lengthwise,
remove the core from each wedge,
then slice.

2 Lay the pineapple slices in a shallow
glass serving bowl. Sprinkle with
confectioners' sugar and drizzle the
orange-flower water over.

COOK'S TIP
Orange-flower water is available at
Middle Eastern food stores or
good delicatessens.

3 Add the dates and strawberries to the
pineapple, cover and chill for at least
2 hours, stirring once or twice. Serve
decorated with a few mint sprigs.

NUTRITIONAL NOTES
Per portion:

Calories	127
Fat, total	0.4g
Saturated fat	0g
Cholesterol	0mg
Fiber	2.9g

ICED PINEAPPLE CRUSH

The sweet tropical flavors of pineapple and lychees combine well with richly scented strawberries to make this a most refreshing salad.

INGREDIENTS

2 small pineapples
4 cups strawberries
1 can (14 ounces) lychees
3 tablespoons kirsch or white rum
2 tablespoons confectioners' sugar

SERVES 4

1 Remove the crown from both pineapples by twisting sharply. Reserve the leaves for decoration.

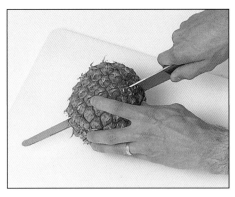

2 Cut the fruit in half diagonally with a large serrated knife.

3 Cut around the flesh inside the skin with a small serrated knife, keeping the skin intact. Remove the core from the pineapple.

4 Chop the pineapple and combine with the strawberries and lychees, taking care not to damage the fruit.

5 Combine the kirsch or rum with the confectioners' sugar, pour over the fruit and freeze for 45 minutes.

6 Turn the fruit out into the pineapple skins and decorate with the pineapple leaves. Serve chilled.

VARIATION

You could use other tropical fruit such as mango, papaya or guava as well as the pineapple.

NUTRITIONAL NOTES

Per portion:

Calories	251
Fat, total	0.7g
Saturated fat	0g
Cholesterol	0mg
Fiber	5.2g

COOK'S TIP

A ripe pineapple will resist pressure when squeezed and will have a sweet, fragrant smell. In winter, freezing conditions can cause the flesh to blacken.

PINEAPPLE WEDGES WITH ALLSPICE AND LIME

Fresh pineapple is easy to prepare and always looks festive, so this dish is
perfect for easy entertaining.

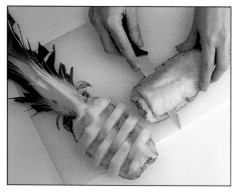

2 Loosen the flesh on each wedge by
sliding a knife between the flesh and the
skin. Cut the flesh into slices, leaving it
on the skin.

3 Using a zester or sharp-pointed knife,
remove a few shreds of zest from the lime.
Squeeze out the juice.

INGREDIENTS
1 ripe pineapple, about 1¾ pounds
1 lime
1 tablespoon dark brown sugar
1 teaspoon ground allspice

SERVES 4

1 Cut the pineapple lengthwise into
quarters and remove the hard core from
each wedge.

4 Sprinkle the pineapple with the lime
juice and zest, sugar and allspice. Serve
immediately, or chill for up to an hour.

NUTRITIONAL NOTES
Per portion:

Calories	96
Fat, total	0.5g
Saturated fat	0.03g
Cholesterol	0mg
Fiber	2.3g

PAPAYA AND MANGO MEDLEY WITH ICED YOGURT

—

Tropical fruit with iced mango yogurt makes a wonderful dessert.
Buy very ripe fruit for this dessert.

INGREDIENTS

2 large ripe mangoes, total weight
about 1 1/2 pounds
1 1/4 cups low-fat
plain yogurt
8 dried apricots, halved
2/3 cup unsweetened
orange juice
1 ripe papaya, about 11 ounces

SERVES 4

1 Take one thick slice from one of the mangoes and, while still on the skin, slash the flesh with a sharp knife in a criss-cross pattern to make cubes.

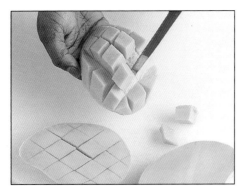

2 Turn the piece of mango inside-out and cut away the cubed flesh from the skin. Place in a bowl, mash to a pulp with a fork, then add the plain yogurt and mix well. Spoon into a freezer tub and freeze for about 1–1 1/2 hours, until half frozen.

3 Meanwhile, put the apricots and orange juice in a small saucepan. Bring to a boil, then simmer gently until the apricots are soft, adding a little water, if necessary, so that the apricots remain moist. Remove from heat and set aside to cool.

4 Peel, pit and chop the remaining mangoes. Halve the papaya, remove seeds and peel. Dice the flesh and add to the mango. Pour the apricot sauce on top.

5 Stir the mango yogurt a few times. Serve the fruit topped with the mango yogurt.

NUTRITIONAL NOTES

Per portion:

Calories	231
Fat, total	4.3g
Saturated fat	2.44g
Cholesterol	5.3mg
Fiber	7.5g

PINEAPPLE AND PASSION FRUIT SALSA

—

Serve this fruity salsa alone or as a filling for halved baby cantaloupes.
Either way it is a cool, refreshing dessert to serve at a dinner party.

INGREDIENTS

1 small fresh pineapple
2 passion fruit
2/3 cup low-fat
plain yogurt
2 tablespoons light brown sugar
meringues, to serve (optional)

SERVES 6

1 Cut off the top and bottom of the pineapple so that it will stand firmly on a chopping board. Using a large sharp knife, slice off the peel.

2 Use a small sharp knife carefully to cut out the eyes from around the pineapple.

VARIATION

Use low-fat fromage frais instead of the yogurt, if you like.

3 Slice the pineapple and use a small pastry cutter to stamp out the tough core from each slice. Finely chop the flesh.

4 Cut the passion fruit in half and scoop out the seeds and pulp into a bowl.

NUTRITIONAL NOTES
Per portion:

Calories	82
Fat, total	1.5g
Saturated fat	0.79g
Cholesterol	1.8mg
Fiber	1.3g

5 Stir in the chopped pineapple and yogurt. Cover and chill.

6 Stir in the brown sugar just before serving the salsa. Serve with meringues, if you like.

GRAPEFRUIT SALAD WITH CAMPARI AND ORANGE

—

The bitter-sweet flavor of Campari combines especially well with citrus fruit
for this sophisticated dessert.

INGREDIENTS
2/3 cup water
3 tablespoons sugar
1/4 cup Campari
2 tablespoons lemon juice
4 grapefruit
5 oranges
4 sprigs fresh mint

SERVES 4

COOK'S TIP
When buying citrus fruit, choose
brightly colored varieties that feel
heavy for their size.

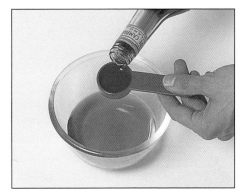

1 Bring the water to a boil in a small
saucepan, add the sugar and simmer until
dissolved. Cool in a metal tray, then add
the Campari and lemon juice. Chill until
ready to serve.

2 Peel the grapefruit and oranges.
Working over a bowl cut the fruit into
sections. Add them to the bowl, stir in the
Campari syrup and chill again.

3 Spoon the salad into four dishes and
finish with a sprig of fresh mint.

NUTRITIONAL NOTES
Per portion:

Calories	182
Fat, total	0.4g
Saturated fat	0g
Cholesterol	0mg
Fiber	5.3g

MUSCAT GRAPE FRAPPÉ

—

The flavor and perfume of the Muscat grape is rarely more enticing than
when captured in this icy-cool salad.

2 Remove the seeds from the grapes with
a pair of tweezers. If you have time, peel
the grapes.

3 Scrape the frozen wine with a
tablespoon to make a fine ice. Combine
the grapes with the ice and spoon into
four shallow glasses.

INGREDIENTS

*1/2 bottle Muscat wine, Beaumes de Venise,
Frontignan or Rivesaltes*

2/3 cup water

4 cups Muscat grapes

SERVES 4

COOK'S TIP

To make this frappé alcohol-free,
substitute 1¹/4 cups apple or grape
juice for the wine.

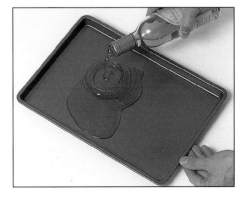

1 Pour the wine into a stainless steel or
nonstick tray, add the water and freeze for
3 hours, or until completely solid.

NUTRITIONAL NOTES

Per portion:

Calories	155
Fat, total	0g
Saturated fat	0g
Cholesterol	0mg
Fiber	1g

COOL GREEN FRUIT SALAD
—

A sophisticated, simple fruit salad, which would look
wonderful served on a bed of crushed ice.

INGREDIENTS

3 Ogen or Galia melons
1 cup green seedless grapes
2 kiwi fruits
1 star fruit, plus extra slices to garnish
1 green-skinned apple
1 lime
³/4 cup unsweetened sparkling grape juice

SERVES 6

3 Thinly pare the zest from the lime and
cut it in fine strips. Blanch the strips in
boiling water for 30 seconds, and then
drain them and rinse them in cold water.
Squeeze the juice from the lime and pour
it over the fruit. Toss lightly.

4 Spoon the prepared fruit into the
reserved melon shells; chill the shells in
the refrigerator until required. Just before
serving, spoon the sparkling grape juice
over the fruit and scatter with lime zest.
Decorate with slices of star fruit.

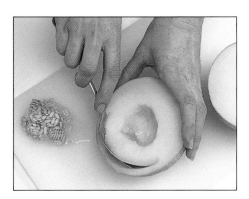

1 Halve the melons and scoop out the
seeds. Keeping the shells intact, scoop
out the flesh and cut into bite-size cubes.
Reserve the melon shells.

2 Cut any large grapes in half. Peel and
chop the kiwi fruits. Slice the star fruit
and set aside a few slices for decoration.
Core and slice the apple and place in a
bowl, with the other fruit.

NUTRITIONAL NOTES
Per portion:

Calories	91
Fat, total	0.4g
Saturated fat	0.00g
Cholesterol	0.0mg
Fiber	1.6g

BLACKBERRY SALAD WITH ROSE GRANITA

The blackberry is a member of the rose family and combines especially well with rose-water.
Here a rose syrup is frozen into a granita and served over strips of white meringue.

INGREDIENTS

2¹/2 cups water
2/3 cup sugar
petals from 1 fresh red rose grown without
pesticides, finely chopped
1 teaspoon rose-water
2 teaspoons lemon juice
4 cups blackberries
confectioners' sugar, for dusting

FOR THE MERINGUE

2 egg whites
1/2 cup sugar
SERVES 4

2 Preheat the oven to 275°F. Line a baking sheet with six layers of newspaper and cover with baking parchment.

4 Spoon the meringue into a piping bag fitted with a ¹/2-inch plain nozzle. Pipe the meringue in lengths across the paper-lined baking sheet. Dry in the bottom of the oven for 1¹/2–2 hours.

1 Bring 2/3 cup of the water to a boil in a stainless steel or enamel saucepan. Add the sugar and chopped rose petals, then lower the heat and simmer for 5 minutes. Strain the syrup into a deep metal tray, add the remaining water, the rose-water and lemon juice; let cool. Freeze the mixture for approximately 3 hours or until solid.

3 Make the meringue. Beat the egg whites in a grease-free bowl until they form soft peaks. Beat in the sugar, a little at a time, then continue to beat until the meringue forms stiff peaks when the beater is lifted.

5 Break the meringue into 2-inch lengths and place three or four lengths on each of four large plates. Pile the blackberries next to the meringue. With a tablespoon, scrape the granita finely. Shape into ovals and place over the meringue. Dust with confectioners' sugar and serve immediately.

NUTRITIONAL NOTES

Per portion:

Calories	310
Fat, total	0.2g
Saturated fat	0g
Cholesterol	0mg
Fiber	3.5g

COOK'S TIP

Serve the dessert as soon as possible after piling the granita on the meringue, or the meringue will become soggy.

VARIATION

Other soft fruits such as blueberries, raspberries or loganberries would work equally well with this dessert.

BLUEBERRY AND ORANGE SALAD MERINGUES

What could be prettier than this simple salad composed of delicate blueberries, sharp oranges and little meringues flavored with lavender?

INGREDIENTS
6 oranges
3 cups blueberries
8 sprigs fresh lavender

FOR THE MERINGUE
2 egg whites
1/2 cup sugar
1 teaspoon fresh lavender flowers

SERVES 4

1 Preheat the oven to 275°F. Line a baking sheet with six layers of newspaper and cover with baking parchment. Beat the egg whites in a large grease-free bowl until they hold soft peaks. Add the sugar a little at a time, beating thoroughly after each addition. Fold in the lavender flowers.

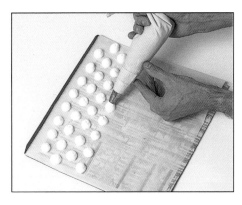

2 Spoon the meringue into a piping bag fitted with a 1/4-inch plain nozzle. Pipe as many small buttons of meringue onto the prepared baking sheet as you can. Dry the meringue near the bottom of the oven for 1 1/2–2 hours.

3 To section the oranges, remove the peel from the top, bottom and sides with a serrated knife. Loosen the sections by cutting with a paring knife between the flesh and the membranes, holding the fruit over a bowl.

4 Arrange the sections on four plates, fanning them out.

5 Combine the blueberries with the lavender meringues and pile in the center of each plate. Decorate with sprigs of lavender and serve immediately.

NUTRITIONAL NOTES
Per portion:

Calories	198
Fat, total	0.3g
Saturated fat	0g
Cholesterol	0mg
Fiber	3.5g

COOK'S TIP
Lavender is used in both sweet and savory dishes. Always use fresh, pesticide-free or recently dried flowers, and avoid artificially scented bunches that are sold for dried flower displays.

VARIATION
You could use blackberries or firm raspberries with fresh rosemary leaves and flowers for this dessert. You could also make 3-inch circles of meringue instead of small buttons and layer the soft fruit in between circles of meringue.

MIXED FRUIT SALAD

—

A really good fruit salad is always refreshing, especially when it comes bathed in fresh orange
and lemon juices. Use any mixture of fresh seasonal fruits.

1 Place the fresh orange and lemon juices
in a large serving bowl.

2 Prepare all the fruits by washing or
peeling them as necessary. Cut them into
bite-size pieces. Halve the grapes and
remove any seeds. Core and slice the
apples. Pit and slice soft fruits and
leave small berries whole. As soon as
each fruit is prepared, add it to the juices
in the bowl.

3 Taste the salad, adding sugar if needed.
Liqueur can also be added, if you like.
Cover the bowl and put it in the
refrigerator for at least 2 hours. Mix well
before serving.

INGREDIENTS

juice of 3 large sweet oranges
juice of 1 lemon
1 banana
1–2 apples
1 ripe pear
2 peaches or nectarines
4–5 apricots or plums
1 cup red or green grapes
1 cup strawberries or raspberries
any other fruits in season
sugar, to taste (optional)
2–3 tablespoons Kirsch, Maraschino or
other liqueur (optional)

SERVES 4

COOK'S TIP

Try adding chopped fresh herbs such
as pineapple mint, lemon balm or
borage flowers, to give a herb-infused
flavor to this fruit salad.

NUTRITIONAL NOTES

Per portion:

Calories	133
Fat, total	0.4g
Saturated fat	0.03g
Cholesterol	0mg
Fiber	3.8g

SPICED FRUIT PLATTER

The spicy sour flavor of chat masala may seem a little strange at first, but this Indian dessert can become quite addictive!

INGREDIENTS

1 pineapple

2 papayas

1 small melon

juice of 2 limes

2 pomegranates

garam masala, to taste

sprigs of fresh mint, to decorate

SERVES 6

NUTRITIONAL NOTES

Per portion:

Calories	102
Fat, total	0.5g
Saturated fat	0g
Cholesterol	0mg
Fiber	4.8g

1 Peel the pineapple. Remove the core and any remaining eyes, then cut the flesh lengthwise into thin wedges. Peel the papayas, cut them in half, and then into thin wedges. Halve the melon and remove the seeds from the middle. Cut it into thin wedges and remove the skin.

2 Arrange the fruit on six individual plates and sprinkle with the lime juice. Cut the pomegranates in half and scoop out the seeds, discarding any pith. Scatter the seeds over the fruit. Serve, sprinkled with a little garam masala to taste. Scatter over a few sprigs of mint, to decorate.

RUBY FRUIT SALAD

After a rich main course, this port-flavored fruit salad is light and refreshing.
Use any fruit that is available.

INGREDIENTS

1¼ cups water

½ cup sugar

1 cinnamon stick

4 cloves

pared zest of 1 orange

1¼ cups port

2 oranges

1 small ripe Ogen, Charentais or
honeydew melon

4 small bananas

2 dessert apples

2 cups seedless grapes

SERVES 8

1 Put the water, sugar, spices and pared orange zest into a pan and stir over a gentle heat to dissolve the sugar. Then bring to a boil, lower the heat, cover and simmer for 10 minutes. Let cool, then add the port.

2 Strain the liquid into a bowl. With a sharp knife, cut off all the skin and pith from the oranges. Then, holding each orange over the bowl to catch the juice, cut it into sections, allowing them to drop into the syrup. Squeeze the remaining pulp to release any juice.

3 Cut the melon in half, remove the seeds and scoop out the flesh or cut it into small cubes. Add it to the syrup.

4 Peel the bananas and cut them diagonally in ½-inch slices. Quarter and core the apples and cut the wedges in small cubes. Leave the skin on, or peel them if it is tough. Halve the grapes if large or leave them whole. Stir all the fruit into the syrup, cover with plastic wrap and chill for an hour before serving.

NUTRITIONAL NOTES

Per portion:

Calories	212
Fat, total	0.2g
Saturated fat	0.04g
Cholesterol	0mg
Fiber	1.9g

WINTER FRUIT SALAD

—

A colorful, refreshing and nutritious fruit salad, this makes an excellent choice
for a winter buffet.

2 Section the oranges, catching any
juice in the bowl, then add the orange
sections and pineapple to the fruit
juice mixture.

3 Core and chop the apples and pears
and add them to the bowl.

4 Stir in the plums, dates and apricots.
Cover and chill for several hours.
Decorate with fresh mint sprigs to serve.

INGREDIENTS

1 can (8 ounces) pineapple cubes in
fruit juice
scant 1 cup fresh orange juice
scant 1 cup unsweetened apple juice
2 tablespoons orange- or
apple-flavored liqueur
2 tablespoons honey (optional)
2 oranges, peeled
2 green-skinned apples
2 pears
4 plums, pitted and chopped
12 fresh dates, pitted and chopped
1/2 cup dried apricots
fresh mint sprigs, to decorate

SERVES 6

1 Drain the pineapple, reserving the juice
in a large serving bowl. Add the orange
juice, apple juice, liqueur and honey, if
using, and stir.

NUTRITIONAL NOTES
Per portion:

Calories	227
Fat, total	0.37g
Saturated fat	0g
Cholesterol	0mg
Fiber	5.34g

MIXED MELON SALAD

—

Several melon varieties are combined with strongly flavored wild or alpine strawberries for a delicious end to a meal.

INGREDIENTS
1 cantaloupe or charentais melon
1 Galia melon
2 pounds watermelon
6 ounces wild strawberries
4 sprigs fresh mint

SERVES 4

1 Cut the cantaloupe and Galia melons and watermelon in half.

2 Using a spoon, scoop out the seeds from the cantaloupe and Galia.

NUTRITIONAL NOTES
Per portion:

Calories	91
Fat, total	0.7g
Saturated fat	0g
Cholesterol	0mg
Fiber	2.7g

3 With a melon scoop, take out as many balls as you can from all three melons. Mix them together in a large bowl, cover and put the bowl in the refrigerator. Chill for 2–3 hours.

4 Just before serving, add the wild strawberries and mix lightly. Spoon into four stem glass dishes.

5 Decorate with sprigs of mint and serve at once.

MARZIPAN FIGS WITH DATES

—

Sweet Mediterranean figs and dates combine especially well with crisp
dessert apples. A hint of almond serves to unite the flavors.

INGREDIENTS
6 large apples
juice of 1/2 lemon
1 cup fresh dates
1 ounce white marzipan
1 teaspoon orange-flower water
1/4 cup low-fat plain yogurt
4 green or purple figs
4 almonds, toasted

SERVES 4

1 Core the apples. Slice thinly, then cut
into fine matchsticks. Moisten with lemon
juice to prevent them from browning.

2 Remove the pits from the dates and cut
the flesh into fine strips, then mix with the
apple slices in a bowl.

3 Soften the marzipan with orange-flower
water and combine with the low-fat
yogurt. Mix well.

4 Pile the apples and dates in the center
of four plates. Remove the stem from each
of the figs and cut the fruit into quarters
without slicing right through the bottom.
Squeeze the bottom with the thumb and
forefinger of each hand to open the fruit.

5 Place a fig in the center of the salad,
spoon in the yogurt filling and decorate
each portion with a toasted almond.

NUTRITIONAL NOTES
Per portion:

Calories	210
Fat, total	3.1g
Saturated fat	0.15g
Cholesterol	0.6mg
Fiber	5.4g

TROPICAL FRUIT SALAD

A glorious medley of tropical fruits, and ginger to add that certain spice. Coconut is a significant source of fat, so go easy on the strips used for decoration.

INGREDIENTS

1 pineapple, about 1 pound 5 ounces
1 can (14 ounces) guava halves in syrup
2 medium bananas, sliced
1 large mango, peeled, pitted and diced
4 ounces preserved ginger, plus 2
tablespoons of the syrup from the jar
4 tablespoons thick coconut milk
2 teaspoons granulated sugar
1/2 teaspoon freshly grated nutmeg
1/2 teaspoon ground cinnamon
a few fine strips of coconut, to decorate

SERVES 4–6

3 Pour 2 tablespoons of the ginger syrup, and the reserved guava syrup, into a blender or food processor. Add the remaining banana slices with the coconut milk and the sugar. Blend to a smooth, creamy purée.

NUTRITIONAL NOTES
Per portion:

Calories	340
Fat, total	1.8g
Saturated fat	0.83g
Cholesterol	0mg
Fiber	8.1g

4 Pour the banana and coconut mixture over the tropical fruit. Add a little grated nutmeg and a sprinkling of cinnamon on the top. Serve chilled, decorated with fine strips of coconut.

1 Peel, core and cube the pineapple, and place in a serving bowl. Drain the guavas, reserving the syrup, and chop. Add the guavas to the bowl with half the sliced banana and the mango.

2 Chop the preserved ginger and add to the pineapple mixture.

MELON AND STRAWBERRY SALAD

—

This colorful fruit salad can be served either as a dessert or as a refreshing appetizer.
Try to find three different colors of melon to serve.

INGREDIENTS

1 Galia melon

1 honeydew melon

1/2 watermelon

2 cups fresh strawberries,
halved if large

1 tablespoon lemon juice

1 tablespoon honey

1 tablespoon water

1 tablespoon chopped fresh mint

SERVES 4

NUTRITIONAL NOTES

Per portion:

Calories	139
Fat, total	0.84g
Saturated fat	0g
Cholesterol	0mg
Fiber	2g

2 Mix the lemon juice, honey and water in a cup. Pour over the fruit and mix.

3 Sprinkle the chopped mint over the fruit and serve.

1 Prepare the melons by cutting them in half and scraping out the seeds. Use a melon baller to scoop out the flesh into balls or a knife to cut it into cubes. Place these in a fruit bowl and add the fresh strawberries.

PAPAYA AND GREEN GRAPES WITH MINT SYRUP

—

Cool, fresh and virtually fat-free, this wonderful combination of textures and flavors makes the
perfect dessert to follow a spicy main course.

INGREDIENTS

2 large papayas

2 cups seedless green grapes

juice of 3 limes

*1-inch fresh ginger root, peeled and
finely grated*

1 tablespoon honey

*5 fresh mint leaves, cut into thin strips,
plus extra whole leaves, to decorate*

SERVES 4

1 Peel the papaya and cut into small
cubes, discarding the seeds. Cut the
grapes in half.

2 In a bowl, mix together the lime juice,
grated ginger root, honey and shredded
mint leaves.

3 Add the papaya and grapes and toss
well. Cover and set aside in a cool place
to marinate for 1 hour.

4 Serve in a large dish or individual stem
glasses, garnished with the whole fresh
mint leaves.

NUTRITIONAL NOTES
Per portion:

Calories	120
Fat, total	0.2g
Saturated fat	0g
Cholesterol	0mg
Fiber	4.4g

PAPAYA SKEWERS WITH PASSION FRUIT COULIS

Tropical fruits, full of natural sweetness, make a simple, exotic dessert.
If you are short of time the passion fruit flesh can be used without puréeing or sieving.

INGREDIENTS

3 ripe papayas
10 passion fruits or kiwi fruits
2 tablespoons fresh lime juice
2 tablespoons confectioners' sugar
2 tablespoons white rum
lime slices, to garnish

SERVES 6

NUTRITIONAL NOTES

Per portion:

Calories	94
Fat, total	0.3g
Saturated fat	0g
Cholesterol	0mg
Fiber	4.1g

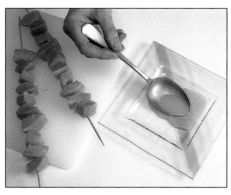

3 Press the fruit pulp through a sieve placed over a bowl; discard the seeds. Add the lime juice, confectioners' sugar and rum, then stir the coulis well until the sugar has dissolved.

4 Spoon a little coulis onto plates and place the skewers on top. Scoop the flesh from the remaining passion fruit or kiwis and spoon over. Garnish with slices of lime and serve immediately.

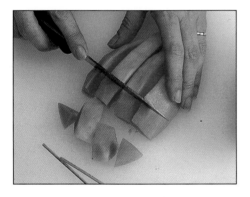

1 Cut the papayas in half and scoop out the seeds. Peel them and cut the flesh into even-size chunks. Thread the chunks on to six bamboo skewers.

2 Halve eight of the passion fruits or kiwis and scoop out the flesh. Purée the flesh for a few seconds in a blender of food processor.

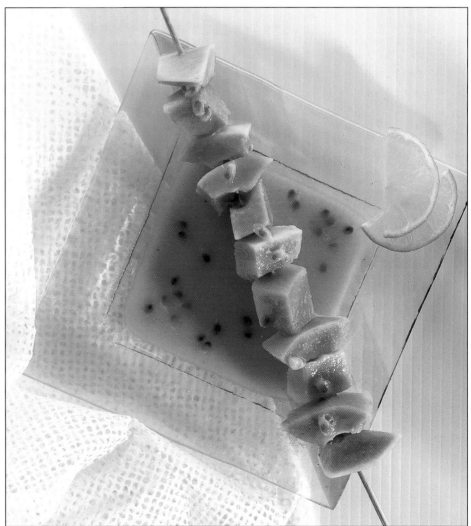

THREE-FRUIT COMPOTE

Mixing dried fruits with fresh ones makes a good combination, especially when they are flavored delicately with a little orange-flower water.

INGREDIENTS
1 cup dried apricots
1¼ cups water
1 small ripe pineapple
1 small ripe melon, about 1 pound
1 tablespoon orange-flower water
mint sprigs, to decorate

SERVES 6

NUTRITIONAL NOTES
Per portion:

Calories	86
Fat, total	0.4g
Saturated fat	0g
Cholesterol	0mg
Fiber	3.2g

2 Peel and quarter the pineapple, then cut the core from each quarter and discard. Cut the flesh into chunks.

3 Cut the melon in half and scrape out the seeds. Working over a bowl to catch the juices, scoop balls from the flesh. Pour the juices into the apricots.

4 Put the apricots, with the soaking juices, into a bowl. Stir in the orange-flower water. Add the pineapple and melon and mix all the fruits gently.

5 Pour into a serving dish or individual dessert dishes. Decorate with a mint sprig and chill lightly before serving.

1 Put the apricots into a saucepan and pour in the water. Bring to a boil, then lower the heat and simmer for 5 minutes. Let cool.

VARIATION
A good fruit salad doesn't have to consist of a mixture of fruits. For a delicious red fruit salad, try berries with sliced plums, or for green fruits, try apples, kiwis and green grapes.

APRICOT AND BANANA COMPOTE

—

This compote is delicious served on its own or with low-fat custard or ice cream. Served for breakfast, it makes a tasty start to the day.

3 Spoon the fruit and juices into a large serving dish.

4 Serve immediately, or cover and chill for several hours first. Sprinkle with flaked almonds just before serving.

INGREDIENTS

1 cup dried apricots
1¹/4 cups orange juice
2/3 cup unsweetened apple juice
1 teaspoon ground ginger
3 medium bananas, sliced
1/4 cup toasted flaked almonds

SERVES 4

1 Put the apricots in a saucepan with the fruit juices and ginger and stir. Cover, bring to a boil and then simmer gently for 10 minutes, stirring occasionally.

2 Set aside to cool, leaving the lid on. Once cool, stir in the sliced bananas.

COOK'S TIP

Use other combinations of dried and fresh fruit such as prunes or figs and apples or peaches.

NUTRITIONAL NOTES

Per portion:

Calories	241
Fat, total	4.18g
Saturated fat	0.37g
Cholesterol	0mg
Fiber	4.91g

SPICED FRUITS JUBILEE

Based on the classic Cherries Jubilee, this is a great way to use up any pitted fruit.
The spiced syrup is a delicious bonus.

2 Add the fruit, cover the pan and simmer for 5 minutes. Drain the fruit and set it aside; return the syrup to the pan. Boil it, uncovered, for 2 minutes or until thick and syrupy.

3 Put the arrowroot in a small bowl and stir in 2 tablespoons of the brandy. Stir the mixture into the syrup. Continue cooking and stirring, until the sauce thickens. Return the fruit to the pan.

4 If serving with ice cream, place a scoop in each serving bowl and spoon the hot fruit over. Warm the remaining brandy in a small pan, then set it alight. Ladle it over the fruit at the table for maximum dramatic effect.

INGREDIENTS

1/2 cup sugar

thinly pared zest of 1 lemon

1 cinnamon stick

4 whole cloves

1 1/4 cups water

8 ounces tart red plums, pitted and sliced

8 ounces nectarines, pitted and chopped

2 cups cherries, pitted

1 teaspoon arrowroot

5 tablespoons brandy

low-fat vanilla ice cream, to serve
(optional)

SERVES 6

1 Put the sugar, lemon zest, cinnamon stick, cloves and water in a pan. Bring to a boil, stirring. Lower the heat and simmer for 5 minutes, then lift out the spices with a slotted spoon and discard.

NUTRITIONAL NOTES
Per portion:

Calories	151
Fat, total	0.1g
Saturated fat	0g
Cholesterol	0mg
Fiber	1g

ITALIAN FRUIT SALAD AND ICE CREAM

If you visit Italy in the summer, you will find little storefront fruit shops selling small dishes of macerated soft fruits, which are delectable on their own, but also make a wonderful ice cream.

INGREDIENTS

8 cups mixed soft fruits, such as strawberries, raspberries, loganberries, red currants, blueberries, peaches, apricots, plums and melons
juice of 6–8 oranges
juice of 1 lemon
1 tablespoon liquid pear and apple concentrate
1/4 cup very low-fat fromage frais
2 tablespoons orange-flavored liqueur (optional)
fresh mint sprigs, to decorate

SERVES 6

1 Prepare the fruit according to type. Cut it into reasonably small pieces, but not so small that the mixture becomes a mush.

2 Put the fruit pieces in a serving bowl and pour over enough orange juice to cover. Add the lemon juice, stir gently, cover and chill for 2 hours.

3 Set half the macerated fruit aside to serve as it is. Purée the remainder in a blender or food processor.

4 Gently warm the pear and apple concentrate and stir it into the fruit purée. Whip the fromage frais and fold it in, then add the liqueur, if using.

NUTRITIONAL NOTES
Per portion:

Calories	60
Fat, total	0.2g
Saturated fat	0.01g
Cholesterol	0.1mg
Fiber	3.2g

5 Churn the mixture in an ice-cream maker. Alternatively, place in a container and freeze it until ice crystals form around the edge. Beat the mixture until smooth. Repeat the process once or twice, then freeze until firm. Soften slightly before serving in scoops decorated with mint accompanied by the macerated fruit.

GINGER AND HONEY SYRUP

—

Particularly good for winter desserts, this virtually fat-free sauce can be served hot or cold
with a variety of your favorite fruit salads.

INGREDIENTS

1 lemon
4 green cardamom pods
1 cinnamon stick
2/3 cup honey
3 pieces preserved ginger, plus
2 tablespoons syrup from the jar
1/4 cup water

SERVES 4

1 Thinly pare two strips of zest from the lemon with a potato peeler.

2 Lightly crush the cardamom pods with the back of a heavy-bladed knife. Cut the lemon in half. Reserve half for another recipe and squeeze the juice from the other half. Set the juice aside.

NUTRITIONAL NOTES

Per portion:

Calories	145
Fat, total	0.1g
Saturated fat	0g
Cholesterol	0mg
Fiber	0g

3 Place the lemon zest, cardamoms, cinnamon stick, honey, ginger syrup and water in a heavy saucepan. Boil, lower heat and simmer for 2 minutes.

4 Chop the ginger and stir it into the sauce with the lemon juice. Pour over a winter fruit salad or try it with a baked fruit compote. Chill to serve.

LEMON AND LIME SAUCE

—

A tangy, refreshing sauce to end a heavy meal, this goes well with pancakes or fruit tarts
and is the ideal accompaniment for a rich orange or mandarin cheesecake.

2 Place all the zest in a pan, cover with
water and bring to a boil. Drain the zest
through a sieve and set it aside.

3 In a small bowl, mix a little sugar with
the arrowroot. Stir in enough water to give
a smooth paste. Heat the remaining water,
pour in the arrowroot, and stir constantly
until the sauce boils and thickens.

INGREDIENTS

1 lemon

2 limes

¹/4 cup sugar

1¹/2 tablespoons arrowroot

1¹/4 cups water

freshly made pancakes, to serve

fresh lemon balm or mint leaves, to decorate

SERVES 4

1 Using a citrus zester, pare the zest
thinly from the lemon and limes. Squeeze
the juice from the fruit.

NUTRITIONAL NOTES

Per portion:

Calories	75
Fat, total	0.1g
Saturated fat	0g
Cholesterol	0mg
Fiber	0g

VARIATION

This sauce can also be made with
orange and lemon zest if you prefer.

4 Stir in the remaining sugar, the citrus
juice and the reserved zest. Serve hot
with freshly made pancakes. Decorate
with lemon balm or mint.

RED CURRANT AND RASPBERRY COULIS

A dessert sauce for the height of summer to serve with light meringues and fruit sorbets.
Make it particularly pretty with a decoration of fresh flowers and leaves.

3 Blend the cornstarch with the orange juice, then stir into the fruit purée. Transfer to a saucepan and bring to a boil, stirring continuously, and cook for 1–2 minutes until smooth and thick. Set aside until cold.

4 Spoon the sauce over each plate. Drip the cream from a teaspoon to make small dots evenly around the edge. Draw a toothpick stick through the dots to form heart shapes. Scoop or spoon sorbet into the middle and decorate with flowers.

INGREDIENTS

2 cups red currants
4 cups raspberries
1/2 cup confectioners' sugar
1 tablespoon cornstarch
juice of 1 orange
2 tablespoons low-fat cream
edible flowers (pesticide-free), to decorate

SERVES 6

1 Strip the red currants from their stalks. Place them in a blender with the sugar and raspberries, and blend to a purée.

2 Press the fruit mixture through a fine sieve into a bowl and discard the seeds and pulp.

NUTRITIONAL NOTES
Per portion:

Calories	81
Fat, total	1.2g
Saturated fat	0.6g
Cholesterol	0mg
Fiber	3.2g

CHRISTMAS CRANBERRY BOMBE

This alternative to Christmas pudding is light and low in fat,
but still very festive and luxurious.

INGREDIENTS
1 cup buttermilk
4 tablespoons low-fat crème fraîche
1 vanilla bean
2 eggs
2 tablespoons honey
2 tablespoons chopped angelica
2 tablespoons mixed peel
2 teaspoons flaked almonds, toasted

FOR THE SORBET CENTER
1¹/2 cups fresh or frozen cranberries
2/3 cup fresh orange juice
finely grated zest of ¹/2 orange
¹/2 teaspoon apple pie spice
¹/4 cup turbinado sugar

SERVES 6

1 Heat the buttermilk, crème fraîche and vanilla bean until the mixture is almost boiling. Remove the vanilla bean.

NUTRITIONAL NOTES
Per portion:

Calories	153
Fat, total	4.6g
Saturated fat	1.58g
Cholesterol	75.5mg
Fiber	1.5g

2 Place the eggs in a heatproof bowl over a pan of hot water and beat until they are pale and thick. Pour in the heated buttermilk in a thin stream, beating hard. Continue beating over the hot water until the mixture thickens slightly.

3 Beat in the honey and set aside to cool. Spoon the mixture into a freezer container and freeze until slushy, then pour into a bowl and stir in the chopped angelica, mixed peel and almonds.

4 Pack into a 5-cup pudding bowl and hollow out the center. Freeze until firm.

5 Meanwhile, make the sorbet center. Put the cranberries, orange juice, zest and spice in a pan and cook gently until the cranberries are soft. Set some cranberries aside for decorating. Add the sugar to the rest, then purée in a food processor until almost smooth, but still with some texture. Let cool.

6 Fill the hollowed-out center of the bombe with the cranberry mixture, smooth over and freeze until firm. To serve, allow to soften slightly at room temperature, then turn out and serve in medium-sized slices, decorated with the reserved cranberries.

SUMMER FRUIT SALAD ICE CREAM

—

**What could be more delicious on a hot summer day than fresh summer fruits,
lightly frozen in this irresistible ice?**

INGREDIENTS

*6 cups mixed soft summer fruit, such as
raspberries, strawberries, black currants
or red currants*

2 eggs

1 cup low-fat plain yogurt

3/4 cup red grape juice

1 tablespoon powdered gelatin

SERVES 6

1 Reserve half the fruit for the
decoration; purée the rest in a food
processor, then sieve it over a bowl to
make a smooth purée.

2 Separate the eggs and beat the yolks
and the yogurt into the fruit purée.

3 Heat the grape juice until almost
boiling, then remove it from heat.
Sprinkle the gelatin over the grape
juice and stir to dissolve the
gelatin completely.

4 Beat the dissolved gelatin mixture into
the fruit purée. Cool, then pour the
mixture into a container that can safely
be used in the freezer. Freeze until half-
frozen and slushy in consistency.

5 Beat the egg whites in a grease-free
bowl until stiff. Quickly fold them into the
half-frozen mixture.

6 Return the ice cream to the freezer and
freeze until almost firm. Scoop into
individual dishes and decorate with the
reserved soft fruits.

VARIATION

You could use other combinations of
summer fruit such as apricots, peaches
and nectarines, with apple or orange
juice for a more delicate ice-cream.

NUTRITIONAL NOTES

Per portion:

Calories	116
Fat, total	3.9g
Saturated fat	1.69g
Cholesterol	66.8mg
Fiber	3.6g

COOK'S TIP

Red grape juice has a good flavor and
improves the color of the ice, but if it is
not available, use cranberry, apple or
orange juice instead.

FROZEN APPLE AND BLACKBERRY TERRINE

—

Apples and blackberries are a classic autumn combination; they really complement each other. This pretty, three-layered terrine can be frozen, so you can enjoy it at any time of year.

INGREDIENTS
1 pound apples
1¼ cups sweet cider
1 tablespoon honey
1 teaspoon pure vanilla extract
scant 2 cups fresh or frozen and
thawed blackberries
1 tablespoon powdered gelatin
2 egg whites
fresh apple slices and blackberries,
to decorate

SERVES 6

1 Peel, core and chop the apples and place them in a pan with half the cider. Bring the cider to a boil, then lower the heat, cover the pan and let the apples simmer gently until tender.

2 Pour the apples into a food processor and process them to a smooth purée. Stir in the honey and vanilla extract. Add half the blackberries to half the apple purée, and process again until smooth. Sieve to remove the seeds.

3 Heat the remaining cider until almost boiling, then sprinkle the gelatin over and stir until the gelatin has dissolved completely. Add half the gelatin mixture to the apple purée and half to the blackberry purée.

4 Set aside both purées to cool until almost set. Beat the egg whites until they are stiff. Quickly fold them into the apple purée. Remove half the purée to another bowl. Stir the remaining whole blackberries into half the apple purée, and then pour this into a 7½-cup loaf pan, packing it down firmly.

5 Top with the blackberry purée and spread it evenly. Finally, add a layer of the plain apple purée and smooth it evenly. If necessary, freeze each layer until firm before adding the next.

6 Freeze until firm. When ready to serve, remove from the freezer and let stand at room temperature for about 20 minutes to soften. Serve in slices, decorated with fresh apple slices and blackberries.

VARIATION
For a quicker version the mixture can be set without the layering. Purée the apples and blackberries together, stir the dissolved gelatin and beaten egg whites into the mixture, turn the whole thing into the pan and let the mixture set.

NUTRITIONAL NOTES
Per portion:

Calories	83
Fat, total	0.2g
Saturated fat	0g
Cholesterol	0mg
Fiber	2.6g

KEY LIME SORBET

Cool and refreshing, this traditional American sorbet is ideal for serving after a curry or similar spicy dish.

INGREDIENTS
1¼ cups sugar
2½ cups water
grated zest of 1 key lime
¾ cup fresh key lime juice
1 tablespoon fresh lemon juice
2 tablespoons confectioners' sugar
key lime shreds, to decorate

SERVES 4

1 In a small heavy saucepan, dissolve the sugar in the water, without stirring, over medium heat. When the sugar has dissolved, boil the syrup for 5–6 minutes. Remove from heat and let cool.

2 Mix the cooled sugar syrup and lime zest and juice in a jug or bowl. Stir well. Sharpen the flavor by adding the lemon juice. Stir in the confectioners' sugar.

3 Freeze the mixture in an ice cream maker, following the manufacturer's instructions. Decorate with lime shreds.

NUTRITIONAL NOTES
Per portion:

Calories	300
Fat, total	0g
Saturated fat	0g
Cholesterol	0mg
Fiber	0g

COOK'S TIP
If you do not have an ice cream maker, pour the mixture into a metal or plastic freezer container and freeze until softly set, about 3 hours. Remove from the container and chop roughly. Process in a food processor until smooth. Return the mixture to the freezer container and freeze again until set. Repeat this process 2 or 3 times, until a smooth consistency is obtained.

RUBY GRAPEFRUIT SORBET

—

On a hot day, nothing is more invigorating than a smooth sorbet.
This one looks as good as it tastes.

INGREDIENTS
¾ cup granulated sugar
½ cup water
4 cups strained freshly squeezed ruby
grapefruit juice
1 tablespoon fresh lemon juice
1 tablespoon confectioners' sugar
mint leaves, to decorate

SERVES 8

1 In a small heavy saucepan, dissolve the granulated sugar in the water over a medium heat, without stirring. When the sugar has dissolved, boil the syrup for 3–4 minutes. Remove from heat and let cool.

2 Pour the cooled sugar syrup into the grapefruit juice. Stir well. Taste the mixture and adjust the flavor by adding the lemon juice or the confectioners' sugar, if necessary, but do not over-sweeten.

3 Pour the mixture into a metal or plastic freezer container and freeze for about 3 hours, or until softly set.

4 Remove from the container and chop roughly into 3-inch pieces. Place in a food processor and process until smooth. Return the mixture to the freezer container and freeze again until set. Repeat this freezing and chopping process 2 or 3 times, until a smooth consistency is obtained.

5 Alternatively, freeze the sorbet in an ice cream maker, following the manufacturer's instructions. Serve, decorated with mint leaves.

NUTRITIONAL NOTES
Per portion:

Calories	133
Fat, total	0.1g
Saturated fat	0g
Cholesterol	0mg
Fiber	0g

MANGO SORBET WITH MANGO SAUCE

After a heavy meal, this Indian speciality makes a very refreshing dessert. Remove from the freezer 10 minutes before serving to allow it to soften and give the full flavor time to develop.

INGREDIENTS

5 cups mango pulp
1/2 teaspoon lemon juice
grated zest of 1 orange and 1 lemon
4 egg whites
1/4 cup granulated sugar
1/2 cup low-fat plain yogurt
1/2 cup confectioners' sugar

SERVES 4

1 In a large, chilled bowl that can safely be used in the freezer, mix half of the mango pulp with the lemon juice and the grated citrus zest.

NUTRITIONAL NOTES
Per portion:

Calories	259
Fat, total	1.7g
Saturated fat	0.79g
Cholesterol	1.8mg
Fiber	5.9g

2 Beat the egg whites in a grease-free bowl until soft peaks form, then fold into the mango mixture, with the sugar. Cover and freeze for at least 1 hour.

3 Remove the sorbet from the freezer and beat again. Transfer to an ice cream container, and freeze until solid.

4 Lightly beat the yogurt with the confectioners' sugar and the remaining mango pulp. Spoon into a bowl and chill for 24 hours. Scoop out individual servings of sorbet and cover each with mango sauce.

LYCHEE AND ELDERFLOWER SORBET

The flavor of elderflowers is famous for bringing out the essence of gooseberries, but what is less well known is how wonderfully it complements lychees.

INGREDIENTS
3/4 cup sugar
1 2/3 cups water
1 1/4 pounds fresh lychees, peeled and pitted
1 tablespoon undiluted elderflower cordial
dessert cookies, to serve (optional)

SERVES 4

NUTRITIONAL NOTES
Per portion:

Calories	249
Fat, total	0.1g
Saturated fat	0g
Cholesterol	0mg
Fiber	0.9g

1 Heat the sugar and water until the sugar has dissolved. Then boil for 5 minutes and add the lychees. Lower the heat and simmer for 7 minutes. Remove from heat and let cool.

2 Purée the fruit and syrup. Place a sieve over a bowl and pour the purée into it. Press through with a spoon.

3 Stir the elderflower cordial into the strained purée, then pour the mixture into a container that is suitable for the freezer. Freeze for approximately 2 hours, until ice crystals start to form around the edges.

4 Remove the sorbet from the freezer and process briefly in a food processor or blender to break up the crystals. Repeat this process twice more, then freeze until firm.

5 Transfer to the refrigerator for 10 minutes to soften slightly before serving in scoops. Crisp dessert cookies can be served with the sorbet, but aren't really necessary. If you do serve them, remember that they will increase the fat content of the dessert.

PLUM AND PORT SORBET

This is a rather grown-up sorbet, but you could use red grape juice
instead of port if you prefer.

INGREDIENTS

*2 pounds ripe red plums, halved
and pitted*
6 tablespoons sugar
3 tablespoons water
3 tablespoons ruby port or red wine
crisp, sweet cookies, to serve (optional)

SERVES 6

1 Put the plums in a pan with the sugar
and water. Stir over gentle heat until the
sugar has melted, then cover and simmer
gently for about 5 minutes, until the fruit
is soft.

2 Place in a food processor and purée
until smooth, then stir in the port or wine.
Cool completely, then pour into a container
that can safely be used in the freezer and
freeze until firm around the edges.

3 Spoon into the food processor and
process until smooth. Return to the
freezer and freeze until solid.

4 Soften slightly at room temperature
then serve in scoops, with sweet cookies,
if you like but they will add fat content.

NUTRITIONAL NOTES
Per portion:

Calories	166
Fat, total	0.25g
Saturated fat	0g
Cholesterol	0mg
Fiber	3.75g

RASPBERRY SORBET WITH A SOFT FRUIT GARLAND

—

This stunning fresh fruit and herb garnish creates a bold border for the scoops of sorbet.
Make the sorbet in an ice-cream maker, if you have one.

INGREDIENTS
3/4 cup sugar
1 cup water
1 pound fresh or thawed
frozen raspberries
strained juice of 1 orange

FOR THE DECORATION
1 bunch mint
selection of soft fruits, including
strawberries, raspberries, redcurrants
and blueberries

SERVES 8

1 Heat the sugar with the water in a saucepan, until dissolved, stirring occasionally. Bring to a boil, then set aside to cool. Purée the raspberries with the orange juice, then press through a sieve to remove any seeds.

2 Mix the syrup with the puréed raspberries and pour into a suitable container for the freezer. Freeze for 2 hours or until ice crystals form around the edges. Beat until smooth, then return to the freezer for 4 hours.

3 About 30 minutes before serving, transfer the sorbet to the refrigerator to soften slightly. Place a large sprig of mint on the rim of a serving plate, then build up a garland, using more sprigs.

4 Leaving the leaves on, cut the strawberries in half. Arrange on the mint with the other fruit. Place the fruits at different angles and link the leaves with strings of red currants. Place scoops of sorbet in the center.

NUTRITIONAL NOTES
Per portion:

Calories	158
Fat, total	0.4g
Saturated fat	0g
Cholesterol	0mg
Fiber	3.4g

BLACK CURRANT SORBET

—

Black currants make a vibrant and intensely flavored sorbet. If not serving immediately,
cover the sorbet tightly and freeze it again, for up to 1 week.

INGREDIENTS
scant 1/2 cup sugar
1/2 cup water
4 cups black currants
juice of 1/2 lemon
1 tablespoon egg white

SERVES 4

1 Mix the sugar and water in a small
saucepan. Heat gently, stirring until the
sugar dissolves, then boil the syrup for
2 minutes. Remove the pan from heat and
set aside to cool.

2 Remove the black currants from their
stalks by pulling them through the tines
of a fork. Wash thoroughly.

3 In a food processor fitted with the metal
blade, process the black currants and
lemon juice until smooth. Alternatively,
chop the black currants coarsely, then add
the lemon juice. Stir in the sugar syrup.

4 Press the purée through a sieve to
remove the seeds.

5 Pour the black currant purée into a
nonmetallic dish that can safely be used
in the freezer. Cover the dish with plastic
wrap or a lid and freeze until the sorbet is
nearly firm, but still slushy.

6 Cut the sorbet into pieces and process
in a food processor until smooth. With the
machine running, add the egg white
through the feeder tube and process until
well mixed. Pour the sorbet back into the
dish and freeze until almost firm. Chop
the sorbet again and process until smooth.
Serve immediately.

NUTRITIONAL NOTES
Per portion:

Calories	132
Fat, total	0g
Saturated fat	0g
Cholesterol	0mg
Fiber	4.1g

MANGO AND LIME SORBET IN LIME SHELLS

—

This richly flavored sorbet looks pretty served in the lime shells, but is also good
served in scoops for a more traditional presentation.

INGREDIENTS

4 large limes
1 ripe mango
1¹/2 teaspoon powdered gelatin
2 egg whites
1 tablespoon sugar
strips of pared lime zest, to decorate

SERVES 4

1 Slice the top and bottom off each lime.
Squeeze out the juice, keeping the shells
intact, then scrape out the shell membrane.

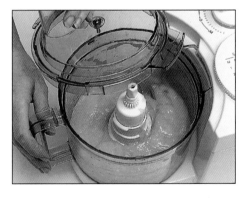

2 Halve, pit, peel and chop the mango.
Purée the flesh in a food processor with
2 tablespoons of the lime juice.

3 Sprinkle the gelatin over
3 tablespoons of the lime juice in a small
heatproof bowl. Set aside until softened,
then place the bowl in a pan of hot water,
stirring occasionally until the gelatine has
dissolved. Stir it into the mango mixture.

4 Beat the egg whites in a grease-free
bowl until they hold soft peaks. Beat
in the sugar. Fold the egg white mixture
quickly into the mango mixture. Spoon
the sorbet into the lime shells. Any
leftover sorbet can be frozen in
small ramekins.

NUTRITIONAL NOTES

Per portion:

Calories	83
Fat, total	0.4g
Saturated fat	0g
Cholesterol	0mg
Fiber	2.3g

5 Place the filled shells in the freezer
until the sorbet is firm. Wrap the shells in
plastic wrap. Before serving, allow the
shells to stand at room temperature for
about 10 minutes; decorate them with
knotted strips of pared lime zest.

WATERMELON SORBET

—

**A slice of this refreshing sorbet is the perfect way to cool down on a hot sunny day.
Ensure the watermelon is perfectly ripe when buying.**

INGREDIENTS

1/2 small watermelon, about 21/4 pounds
6 tablespoons sugar
1/4 cup unsweetened cranberry
juice or water
2 tablespoons lemon juice
sprigs of fresh mint, to decorate

SERVES 6

1 Cut the watermelon into six equal-size wedges. Scoop out the pink flesh, discarding the seeds but reserving the shell.

2 Select a bowl that is about the same size as the melon and which can safely be used in the freezer. Line it with plastic wrap. Arrange the melon skins in the bowl to re-form the shell, fitting them together snugly so that there are no gaps. Put in the freezer.

3 Mix the sugar and cranberry juice or water in a saucepan and stir over a low heat until the sugar dissolves. Bring to a boil, then lower the heat and simmer for 5 minutes. Set aside the sugar syrup to cool.

4 Put the melon flesh and lemon juice in a blender and process to a smooth purée. Stir in the sugar syrup and pour into a freezer-proof container. Freeze for 3–3 1/2 hours, or until slushy.

5 Pour the sorbet into a chilled bowl and beat to break up the ice crystals. Return to the freezer for another 30 minutes, beat again, then pour into the melon shell and freeze until solid.

6 Carefully remove the sorbet-filled melon shell from the freezer and turn it upside down. Use a sharp knife to separate the sections, then quickly place them on individual plates. Decorate with mint sprigs and serve.

NUTRITIONAL NOTES

Per portion:

Calories	125
Fat, total	0.52g
Saturated fat	0g
Cholesterol	0mg
Fiber	0.26g

COOK'S TIP

Watermelon seeds make a delicious and nutritious snack if toasted in a moderate oven until brown and hulled to remove the outer shell.

RHUBARB AND ORANGE WATER ICE

—

Pretty pink rhubarb, with sweet oranges and honey—the perfect summer ice. If needed, add a
little more honey or sugar to taste.

INGREDIENTS

12 ounces pink rhubarb
1 orange
1 tablespoon honey
1 teaspoon powdered gelatin
orange slices, to decorate

SERVES 4

NUTRITIONAL NOTES

Per portion:

Calories	38
Fat, total	0.1g
Saturated fat	0g
Cholesterol	0mg
Fiber	2g

3 Heat the remaining orange juice and
stir in the gelatin to dissolve. Stir it into
the rhubarb. Pour the whole mixture into
a rigid container that can safely be used
in the freezer; freeze for about 2 hours or
until slushy.

4 Remove the mixture from the freezer,
pour into a bowl and beat well to break up
the ice crystals. Return to the freezer
until firm. Soften slightly at room
temperature before serving in scoops,
decorated with orange slices.

1 Trim the rhubarb and slice into
1-inch lengths. Place the rhubarb in a
nonreactive pan.

2 Finely grate the zest from the orange
and squeeze out the juice. Add about half
the orange juice and the grated zest to the
rhubarb in the pan and simmer until the
rhubarb is just tender. Stir in the honey.

ORANGE ICE WITH STRAWBERRIES

—

Juicy oranges and really ripe strawberries make a flavorful ice that does not need
any additional sweetening.

INGREDIENTS
6 large juicy oranges
3 cups ripe strawberries
finely pared strips of orange zest,
to decorate

SERVES 4

NUTRITIONAL NOTES
Per portion:

Calories	124
Fat, total	0.4g
Saturated fat	0g
Cholesterol	0mg
Fiber	5.6g

1 Squeeze the juice from the oranges and
pour into a shallow freezer-proof bowl.
Place the bowl in the freezer. When ice
crystals form around the edge of the
mixture beat the mixture thoroughly.
Repeat this process at 30-minute
intervals over a 4-hour period.

2 Halve the strawberries and arrange
them on a serving plate. Scoop the ice
into serving glasses, decorate with strips
of orange zest and serve immediately with
the strawberries.

COOK'S TIP
The ice will keep for up to 3 weeks in
the freezer. Sweet ruby grapefruits or
deep red blood oranges can be used for
a different flavor and color.

ICED ORANGES

—

These tasty little sorbets served in a fruit shell look impressive and are easy to eat—just the
thing for serving at a barbecue or patio picnic.

NUTRITIONAL NOTES
Per portion:

Calories	167
Fat, total	0.3g
Saturated fat	0g
Cholesterol	0mg
Fiber	4.3g

3 Grate the zest of the six remaining
oranges and add this to the syrup.
Squeeze the juice from the oranges, and
from the reserved flesh. There should be
3 cups. Add water, if necessary.

4 Stir the orange juice into the syrup,
with the remaining lemon juice and water.
Pour the mixture into a shallow container
that can safely be used in the freezer.
Freeze for 3 hours.

5 Place the mixture in a bowl, and beat to
break down the ice crystals. Return
to the freezer container and freeze for
4 hours more, until firm, but not solid.

6 Pack the mixture into the orange shells,
mounding it up, and set the "hats" on top.
Freeze until ready to serve. Just before
serving, make a hole in the top of each
"hat," using a skewer, and push in a bay
leaf as decoration.

INGREDIENTS
2/3 cup granulated sugar
juice of 1 lemon
scant 1 cup water
14 oranges
8 fresh bay leaves, to decorate

SERVES 8

1 Put the sugar in a heavy pan. Add half
the lemon juice, then pour in 1/2 cup of
the water. Heat gently, stirring
occasionally, until the sugar has
dissolved, then bring to a boil, and boil
for 2–3 minutes, until the syrup is clear.
Let cool.

2 Slice the tops off eight of the oranges,
to make "hats". Scoop out the flesh from
inside each, taking care not to damage
the shell, and set it aside. Put the
empty orange shells and the "hats" on
a baking sheet and place in the freezer
until needed.

COOK'S TIP
Use crumpled foil to keep the shells
upright on the baking sheet.

FRESH ORANGE GRANITA

A granita is like a water ice, but coarser and grainy in texture, hence its name.
It makes a refreshing dessert after a rich main course.

INGREDIENTS

4 large oranges

1 large lemon

2/3 cup sugar

2 cups water

dessert cookies, to serve (optional)

pared strips of orange and lemon zest,

to decorate

SERVES 6

1 Thinly pare the orange and lemon zest, avoiding the white pith, and set aside for the decoration. Cut the fruit in half and squeeze the juice into a cup. Set aside.

2 Heat the sugar and water in a heavy saucepan, stirring, until the sugar dissolves. Bring to a boil, then boil without stirring until a syrup forms. Remove the syrup from heat, add the pieces of orange and lemon zest and shake the pan. Cover and let cool.

3 Strain the sugar syrup into a shallow freezer container and add the fruit juice. Stir well to mix, then freeze, uncovered, for about 4 hours, until slushy.

COOK'S TIP

To make the decoration, slice extra orange and lemon zest into thin strips. Blanch for 2 minutes, refresh under cold water and dry before use.

---

4 Remove the half-frozen mixture from the freezer and mix with a fork, then return to the freezer and freeze again for 4 hours more, or until frozen hard.

5 To serve, turn into a bowl and let soften for about 10 minutes, then break up again and pile into long-stem glasses. Decorate with the strips of orange and lemon zest. Serve with dessert cookies, if you like, but remember to take their fat content into account.

NUTRITIONAL NOTES

Per portion:

Calories	139
Fat, total	0.2g
Saturated fat	0g
Cholesterol	0mg
Fiber	1.6g

LEMON GRANITA

Nothing is more refreshing on a hot summer's day
than a fresh lemon granita.

INGREDIENTS

2 cups water

1/2 cup sugar

2 large lemons

SERVES 4

NUTRITIONAL NOTES

Per portion:

Calories	114
Fat, total	0g
Saturated fat	0g
Cholesterol	0mg
Fiber	0g

1 In a large saucepan, heat the water and sugar together over a low heat until the sugar dissolves. Bring to a boil, stirring occasionally. Remove from heat and set aside to cool.

2 Grate the zest from one lemon, then squeeze the juice from both. Stir the grated zest and juice into the sugar syrup. Place it in a shallow container or freezer tray, and freeze until solid.

3 Plunge the bottom of the frozen container or tray in very hot water for a few seconds. Turn the frozen mixture out, and chop it into large chunks.

4 Place the mixture in a food processor fitted with metal blades, and process until it forms small crystals. Spoon into serving glasses.

COFFEE GRANITA

This granita is a cross between a frozen drink and a flavored ice, and can be made at home with the help of a food processor. The consistency should be slushy, not solid.

INGREDIENTS

2 cups water

1/2 cup sugar

1 cup very strong espresso coffee, cooled

SERVES 4

NUTRITIONAL NOTES

Per portion:

Calories	115
Fat, total	0g
Saturated fat	0g
Cholesterol	0mg
Fiber	0g

1 Heat the water and sugar together gently until the sugar dissolves. Bring to a boil, stirring occasionally. Remove from heat and set aside to cool.

2 Stir the coffee and sugar syrup together. Place it in a container and freeze until solid. Plunge the bottom of the frozen container or tray in very hot water. Turn the mixture out, and chop into chunks.

3 Place the mixture in a food processor fitted with metal blades, and process until it forms small crystals. Spoon into tall glasses and serve.

COOK'S TIP

If you do not want to serve the granita immediately, pour the processed mixture back into a shallow container and freeze again. Allow to thaw for a few minutes before serving.

INDEX